Welcome

Welcome to the start of a wonderful journey. When you reach the end of this book you will have discovered a new insight into your actions and behaviours. You will have a new understanding of interpersonal skills and have the ability to positively affect your personal and professional relationships.

DFLeap

DISCovering Your Style
and dealing with difficult people

Derek E Fox

DF-Leap

www.DFLeap.com
info@dfleap.com
© 2011 DF-Leap

All images provided by Graham Ogilvie

http://www.ogilviedesign.co.uk/

Content:

For Denise, Charlie, Andrea, Phyllis, Dave, Noel, Debbie, Pat and Ray. Thank you for encouraging me.

Chapter one: What is DISC

The history, model, and usage of DISC

1

What is DISC?

DISC is a wonderful tool that will provide you with a powerful insight in to your own behaviours and the behaviours of others.

DISC is a personal development tool used by over 40 million people worldwide to improve their success at work, develop their communications, and promote teamwork. The DISC tool focuses on people's strengths and is non-judgemental, it helps people understand and discuss their behavioural differences. DISC will help you identify and understand the impact of your own behaviours and the behaviours of others. Through applying a common language people can gain a greater understanding of interpersonal relationships and behaviours in the workplace.

DISC is an acronym that stands for **D**ominance, **I**nfluence, **S**teadiness, and **C**onscientiousness, which describes the four dimensions of human behaviour. Each of these four dimensions will be discussed later in this chapter.

The History of DISC
'from a concept to a theory and then to a tool'

William Marston

The DISC model can be traced back to the early 1920s where the conceptual work of Dr William Moulton Marston around human behaviour led to the publication of his 1928 book *emotions of normal people*. The book explained his theory on how normal human emotions lead to behavioural differences among different people and how a person's behaviour might change over time depending on their situation and human development. Marston earned his Ph.D. from the prestigious Harvard University; he was a well renowned and well respected psychologist in his field. Marston led an interesting life, he was a qualified lawyer, a psychologist, invented the first functional lie detector known as the polygraph, published several books on emotions and self-help, and also was the creator of the popular comic book character wonder woman.

Marston was born in 1893, and by 1915 he had constructed the first lie detector known as the polygraph. Marston had discovered a relationship between blood pressure and when people told a lie. His device measured changes in a person's blood pressure when the subject was being questioned. He published his first research results in 1917. During the 1920s and 30s Marston was an active lecturer and consultant with various government groups, unlike many other psychologists of the time he was more interested in the behaviour of the general population (normal people) than on abnormal behaviour through clinical psychology. In 1941 all-star comics featured a new character called wonder woman. Marston created this character to act as a role model for young girls across the world.

Marston's work around the DISC model focused on the theory that the behavioural expression of emotions could be categorised into four basic primary types, emerging from the person's perceptions of self in relationship and to their environment. He labelled these four types as dominance (D), inducement (I), submission (S), and compliance (C).

Marston himself did not create a development tool or assessment profile around his DISC model; it was Walter V Clark in 1948 who first started work on developing a assessment tool based on Marston's DISC model. In 1956 he published the *activity vector analysis*, a checklist of words which people were asked to mark the descriptors they identified as being true for themselves. The labels Clark gave to his four constructs were aggressive, sociable, stable and avoidant, and were based on Marston's model.

Clark's work led Dr John Gerier to release the personal profile system® (PPS) in the 1970s. The PPS model gave birth to the tool we know today as DISC but unlike Marston's original labels DISC today stands for Dominance, Influence, Steadiness, and Conscientiousness.

Marston's original work was never copyrighted hence it has led to a number of international providers offering DISC tools and assessments across the globe. The DISC model is one of the most popular models in use across businesses today, its application ranges from profiling potential hiring candidates to helping employees increase their understanding and knowledge of human behaviour around communications, conflict, teamwork, delegation and management.

Nearly 100 years after Marston originally conceptualised the model, DISC is being applied in organisations all across the world helping people achieve greater results through knowledge and understanding of human behaviours.

The Model

Here we will introduce the DISC model and look at the basic understanding of Dominance, Influence, Steadiness and Conscientiousness. In the following chapters we will then look at each of these four behavioural types/factors in more depth.

The DISC model identifies your level of each one of the behavioural factors, whether you are a high or low D for dominance, a high or low I for influence, a high or low S for steadiness, or a high or low C for conscientiousness. The DISC model will show you your blended style across all four behaviour factors. Less than 2% of the population are what is known as a pure style, i.e. a person that is high in only one behaviour factor and low in the other three. For the purpose of introduction and to help you understand the DISC model we will focus on initially describing the basic behaviour factors of the DISC model. As your knowledge and understanding develops you can start to look at blended styles across all four behavioural factors, for example what does someone with a high D and high I look like versus someone that has a high D, low I and high S etc.

The Basic Model

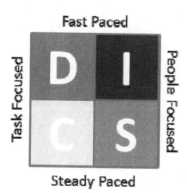

The basic model works across two dimensions. The first dimension looks at your pace, either fast-paced or steady-paced. The second dimension looks at your focus, either task focused or people focused. Depending on your pace and focus this will direct you towards D, I, S or C.

Someone who is both fast-paced and task focused can be described as a high D for dominance. Someone who is fast-paced and people focused can be described as a high I for influence. Someone who is steady paced and task focused can be described as a high C for conscientiousness. Someone who is steady paced and people focused can be described as a high S for steadiness.

Very quickly you can take a look at someone's behaviours and diagnose their pace and focus to identify which behavioural style best describes their behaviour whether it be D, I, S, or C.

D –Dominance

We can describe a person who is fast-paced and task focused as a high D for dominance. A high D can be described as:

- *Results orientated*
- *Goal focused*
- *Action orientated*
- *Decisive and direct*

A person with a high D factor likes to achieve results, has a desire to take control, and is very competitive. They are very comfortable accepting challenges, they can be strong willed and impatient. They are quick to take action and are very innovative. High D's have a tendency to love power and authority, they also have a preference for direct answers. They may have high egos and drive hard for results. They like challenges and are natural problem solvers. Their strong focus on results may be seen by others as overly aggressive behaviour and some D's may be described as being a bully or being too directive when dealing with others.

I –Influence

We can describe a person who is fast-paced and people focused as a high I for influence. A high I can be described as:

- *People orientated*
- *Optimistic and encouraging*
- *Enthusiastic and open*
- *Expressive and outgoing*

A person with a high I factor likes to receive recognition and praise; they are influential and enthusiastic towards their tasks and goals. They may be described as very entertaining and expressive; they can be very talkative and enjoy dealing with people. High I's can be described as socially and verbally aggressive, they are energising and help motivate others. A high I can be seen as overly dependent on interaction with other people and seem overly needy of recognition and praise.

S –Steadiness

We can describe a person who is steady paced and people focused as a high S for steadiness. A high S can be described as:

- *Stable and cooperative*
- *Good listener, sympathetic*
- *Good team worker, dependable*
- *Diplomatic and consistent*

A person with a high S factor likes to avoid conflict and will always seek harmony. They can be described as very loyal to those they identify with, they are good listeners and very patient with others. They dislike rapid or constant change, preferring instead to focus on security and stability.

They like to work within a predictable environment, preferring to work in an environment where traditional and steady procedures are adopted. They have an orientation towards family activities and values. They may procrastinate over decision-making and will avoid giving constructive feedback.

C –Conscientiousness

We can describe a person who is steady paced and task focused as a high C for conscientiousness. A high C can be described as:

- *Analytical and accurate*
- *Orderly and disciplined*
- *Quality conscious*
- *Deliberate and systematic*

A person with a high C factor likes to reflect on situations before taking action. They want to analyse the facts and figures or pros and cons of the situation before making a decision. They are objective thinkers with a tendency to be perfectionists. They set high standards and are well disciplined in delivering accurate results in line with expectations, processes, and/or procedures. They are motivated by the right way to proceed, and will always seek justice in a given situation. The high C's may be seen as cold and withdrawn by others.

These four basic factors of D, I, S, and C make up the DISC behavioural model. Each of the factors has their own unique traits and strengths that will define their individual behavioural style.

Usage of DISC

The DISC model can be applied across a range of business situations such as:

- *Communications*
- *Management*
- *Team development*
- *Conflict resolution*
- *Diversity*
- *Decision-making*

Organisations across the world use the DISC model to help develop both their individual team members and managers to help them achieve their business results and personal goals. As the DISC model focuses on individual strengths and is non-judgemental, the common language can help provide a baseline of communications and promote education and the understanding of different behaviour styles.

There is no right or wrong style, no style is good or bad, they are just different. DISC helps us understand these differences and tap into the potential that these differences can provide us in overcoming challenges and achieving our goals. Here are just a few of the areas where DISC has helped organisations and businesses achieve greater results and reduce potential conflict:

Communications

With a common language DISC helps us understand the strengths and requirements across each of the four behavioural factors. Having a deeper knowledge and understanding of what people need and how they like to receive information will contribute to better interpersonal communications.

Simply knowing that the high D wants quick answers, bullet-pointed information, and high level detail, whereas the high C wants detailed information, facts and figures, and time to reflect on data before making a decision will help you craft your communications more successfully.

Conflict

By providing an understanding of the differences between the four factors DISC helps us understand the source of potential conflict, for example the high I needs acknowledgement and appreciation for their contribution whereas the high D may only believe praise is due when the result is achieved. The high C may become frustrated and agitated when others seem to be cutting corners or taking shortcuts. The high S, while trying to please everyone may frustrate others who see them as unassertive or non-decisive. By understanding the behavioural styles of DISC we can identify the sources of conflict and through education and understanding help individuals and teams work together more efficiently and effectively.

Diversity

By tapping into the range of behaviours across the different four styles we are creating an environment where diversity thrives. By acknowledging and encouraging the broad range of behaviours individuals and teams gain access to more ideas and resources then by simply enforcing one set of rigid rules and regulations for all. When individuals are allowed to express themselves in an environment where their behaviours are encouraged and supported for the added value and strengths that they bring not only is diversity enhanced but innovation is also promoted.

Management

Managers can also benefit from the knowledge and understanding of the DISC model to help them deal more effectively with their staff and team members. Knowing and understanding how to approach and manage a high D, I, S, or C will greatly improve the potential for achieving results through people. When a manager is aware of their own personal style and the potential impact, both positively and negatively on others they can choose to modify and adapt their behaviour to best suit the situation they are faced with. Managerial tasks such as goal setting, motivation and delegation become more effective as the manager adapts their style to suit the individual and/or the situation. DISC also helps with managing upwards and across the organisation by providing managers with a tool to help them diagnose individuals and situations and then select the appropriate behaviour style that will help them achieve success for that given situation.

Team development

Team members can use DISC to help in the development and dynamics of the team. Applying DISC to team development situations such as forming-storming-norming-performing will help teams develop toward success faster. Knowing and understanding why a specific team member acts in a particular way will help the team identify and address unwanted behaviours that may limit their success. Having the ability to understand the positive intent behind individuals' behaviours will remove the potential of this behaviour causing conflict within the team, now the team can simply address the specific behaviour and discuss the potential impact the behaviour will have on other team members.

Individuals

DISC is a practical tool, it can help you increase your self-knowledge in areas such as how you respond to conflict, what motivates you, what causes you stress, and how you solve problems. This will help you learn how to adapt your style and behaviours to get along with others more effectively and achieve results quicker. You can foster constructive and creative group interactions where problems are challenged and results are identified. You can facilitate better interpersonal relationships and minimise potential conflict. Develop stronger internal and external sales orientation skills by identifying and responding to customers styles whether that is inter-department or with external customers.

These are just a few of the positive ways in which DISC can be used within the workplace to help you achieve greater results faster and with less stress or hassle than before. By adopting and applying DISC you will be taking the first steps towards continued success for both you and your organisation.

The essence of DISC is around practising the three A's of enlightenment:

- Acknowledging people are different
- Accepting these differences
- Appreciating these differences

To help you build on these 3A's we will now take a closer look at each of the behavioural styles/factors found within the DISC model.

Chapter Two: Introducing the D-Style

Dominance – Fast-Paced & Task Focused.

2

Introducing the D-Style

With a fast pace and a focus on task, the high D delivers on results and achieves goals through their direct style and behaviour.

The first behaviour factor of the DISC model we will look at is that of the D for dominance behaviour style. As discussed in chapter 1, for the purpose of education and understanding we will focus on a pure D style. Later in this book we will look at blended styles, but for now let's have an introduction to the D behavioural style. We will look at their associated strengths, weaknesses, behavioural traits, and examples of how they behave in certain situations, such as in conflict, when influencing, in communications, and when managing or being managed. Remember where the D style is found on the disc map, their focus is on task and their pace is fast.

An Introduction to the D Style:

People with the behavioural traits of a D style may be generally described by the following attributes:

- self-reliant
- calculated risk taker
- creative problem solver
- results orientated
- challenge driven.

People with a high D style often exhibit behaviours such as activeness in dealing with problems and challenges, not only can they be described as a risk taker, forceful, demanding, domineering, daring, direct, and egocentric, but also as bullying, impatient, pushy, and relentless when they are not getting their own way. People with a high D style tend to have high egos, they enjoy challenges and drive hard for results. They have a positive attitude towards tasks and goals in the workplace. They are motivated by direct answers and seek fast action to complete tasks and resolve issues. They see problems and issues as challenges and will actively go after situations where they can take control and make decisions.

The D style person tries to shape their environment by overcoming opposition and challenges, they enjoy getting immediate results, taking action, and challenging others directly. They are motivated by challenges, goals, power and authority, and direct answers. Their biggest fear is the loss of control in their environment, or being taken advantage of.

When observing a D style you will notice high self-confidence, decisiveness, and risk-taking behaviours. You will also notice a lack of concern for others, impatience, and forcefulness when dealing with others.

In the workplace the D style can bring the following strengths to a team or group:

- they can make decisions when others cannot
- they can confront tough issues or situations
- they can accept change as a personal challenge
- they can keep the team focused and on track.

On the downside they may come across as unapproachable, can be insensitive to others, and may be impatient when others are not showing the same level of urgency in achieving the result as they themselves do. The D style may also try to move the team on before it is ready.

How to recognise the D style:

The D style will appear highly extroverted with a focus on task and come across as very direct in their interactions with others. They will be impatient and set many goals as they are geared towards and look for results and efficiency. In conflict situations they will give as good as they get as their natural response is to fight back. They thrive in a change situation and like to take charge. They may tend to break the rules from time to time with their focus on achieving the result as quickly as possible.

A Typical D in the Workplace:

The D style person tends to be a very strong willed individual who constantly seeks out new challenges. They are typically extremely self-reliant and independent in both thoughts and actions. They prefer to work out their own solutions, although they may ask others for input this will be limited to information, as they rarely seek opinions or solutions from others. The D style person is highly independent and self-sufficient and will always seek to be in control of situations. They respond well to direct instructions that have a focus on output and action. They are very creative and can overcome issues and challenges through applying innovative solutions.

As the D style person is constantly looking for new challenges and opportunities they may be anxious to test new skills and knowledge against the demands that a new situation will place them in. They also have a tendency to believe their way is the best way and may be somewhat reluctant to acknowledge their shortcomings or errors directly. They may tend to keep trying new solutions or approaches until they obtain the results they desire, and in doing so be forceful and pushy with others who do not agree with their way of seeing things.

The D style person is constantly active and is motivated by a sense of urgency and importance. They may easily become bored or frustrated when tasks are routine, tedious, long-term, or slow to achieve results. They enjoy getting an activity or project started and can then hand over the completion to others; however, they tend to want to have complete control for the results of any of the activities or projects for which they are held responsible or which are important to them. Although they are generally very direct and forceful, the D style person may be capable of careful planning and strategic manipulation of people and situations to ensure that their goals are met.

The D style person will have a high expectation of others that work with them and can be critical of people when they do not meet the high standards that they set. They enjoy working with others that are similar to them and display behaviours such as being: self starters, goal orientated, results focused. With their strong focus on results they may seem to lack empathy or understanding of others and can come across as uncaring. The D style person will put their interests first and may appear very self-centred. They are highly motivated by opportunities for personal advancement or achievement. The D style person will become very direct and even possibly aggressive when others stand in their way of achieving results. They can work comfortably within a group or on their own depending on the situation as long as the focus is on achieving results.

When working within a team the D style person will want to take control and make decisions. They can be over forceful and want others to take action quickly before they may have made up their own minds. If the team is not achieving the desired results the D style person will become frustrated and may seek to take full control including micromanaging the activities of others. They will be direct and blunt with feedback tending to focus on the negative aspects of others behaviours and criticising colleagues for not achieving the desired results.

Due to their fast-paced style the D person may not enjoy detailed planning and/or routine documentation. They will only take time to get additional facts or information if there is an obvious lack of information that is limiting their ability to achieve results. Their reporting style will be short and sweet, focusing just on the critical information and the results achieved.

What a D Wants:

The D style person is motivated by having control over their work environment and activities. They also enjoy being able to direct tasks and other people's activities to achieve their goals. They like being offered new opportunities and new challenges to test their skills and abilities. They thrive in situations where they are held personally accountable solely for the results achieved rather than for how the results are achieved. They are always looking for opportunities for advancement and recognition of their ability to achieve success, and they enjoy rewards for achieving their goals.

The D style person wants a work environment which provides maximum freedom to determine how things will be done and there is a focus on fast-pace and results orientation. They demand a working environment where performance measurements and rewards are based upon achieving agreed results. They want to work within situations where they have the opportunity to direct and control the activities and the input of others. They like to be recognised for their ability to lead teams to success and achieve results.

They want to avoid situations where they have no control over their environment or task objectives. They do not like to be put in a situation where they may appear soft or weak. They dislike being closely managed by others or working in situations where routine and predictable behaviours are required day after day.

The D style person wants to work on activities where they are not required to check in frequently and report what they are doing as they dislike reporting step-by-step on how things are going with a task or activity. They also want to work in an environment where resources are available when required and they are not delayed or restricted in achieving their goals.

How a D Likes to do Things:

In this section we will look at how the D style person prefers to do things such as; how they like to communicate, how they like to make decisions, how they manage their time, their approach to problem-solving, how they deal with stress, and how they approach conflict situations.

Communications

The D style person prefers to communicate in a direct and factual manner focusing on the bottom line. They tend to avoid wasting time on small talk or social niceties and will rarely enter into a conversation involving emotions and/or personal feelings. When communicating they have a tendency to tell others what to do without being asked to do so. Sometimes they may be so direct and forceful in communicating that others have difficulty asking them questions or clarifying understanding. Due to this very direct style others may find it difficult to point out issues or problems fearing how the D style may respond. Due to their brief communication style they may be perceived by others as blunt, cold, or uncaring. They will have a difficulty expressing positive emotions even though they may feel them and will automatically assume that others know how they feel, especially if they told them once in the past. The D style person is very comfortable in expressing anger, sometimes using anger or aggression when sadness, hurt or fear would be a more appropriate expression of their true emotional state.

When communicating they tend to be impatient and can have difficulty listening to long discussions and detailed information, preferring to get straight to the point. They have a tendency to be selective listeners, only hearing and storing information as they see it. They will regularly use a judgemental or an evaluative listening style, listening long enough only to make a decision whether they agree or disagree and then they stop listening. They will regularly interrupt or cut across people in conversations to get their own point across. If they think others are not listening to them they may become more forceful or even raise their voice to ensure that they are heard.

Decision-making

The D's style approach to decision-making tends to be quick, decisive, independent and firm. They focus on the bottom line, assessing the short-term impact of the decisions. They may tend to take higher risks than are comfortable for others, believing that the potential for big payoffs will justify the associated risks taken. They may lose sight of the big picture and fail to consider long-term consequences of their actions while focusing on the short-term gains. They may fail to look through all of the information or indicators and not think through all of the factors in complex situations. Once they have reached a decision they become very inflexible and unwilling to change as they believe their decision is correct. They may force decisions through even when others do not agree with their approach or methodology.

Time management

The D style person will operate with a sense of high urgency, taking shortcuts wherever possible to achieve their goals. They strive for efficient solutions that allow them to pack a lot into a single day. They constantly underestimate the time required for some activities, resulting in cutting things short and/or potentially missing deadlines. They are highly critical of others who do not share the same sense of urgency or move at the same fast-pace. They have a tendency to be impatient with others who desire a more leisurely pace. The D's overall approach to time management is 'just do it now' and this applies to both themselves and others. They avoid using complex time management tools and prefer to focus on short to-do lists containing urgent and important short-term goals.

Problem-solving

The D style prefers to use simple, practical, and easy to implement solutions. They avoid detailed or complex problem-solving techniques relying on their tried and trusted methods that have delivered success in the past. They prefer to solve problems independently of others and may have difficulty involving others in the problem-solving process because of their impatience and desire for immediate results. The D style is always looking for the easiest way to overcome an issue or challenge and therefore may implement a solution without thinking about long-term impact. A lot of their solutions are short-term fixes and they are comfortable with just applying a 'Band-Aid' to problem-solving so they can achieve the results. They are not interested in, or want to take the time to develop long-term solutions unless they are forced to do so.

Stress

Because the D style person tends to seek out demanding, challenging, fast-paced environments they may not notice the negative impact on their health or relationships. They tend to perceive the environment as being somewhat antagonistic, requiring an aggressive or defensive stance to given situations. Their biggest source of stress maybe their own strong drive to achieve results that leads them to set unrealistic goals for themselves and others. Another situation the D style will find very stressful is when working in an environment where they do not have control over their activities. They may push themselves too hard and not take adequate time to recover. They may have a tendency to ignore stress and become more forceful and directing when dealing with others. Their need to get things done can cause them to take on too much work and set unrealistic deadlines.

Conflict

In a conflict situation the D style will take a direct and aggressive approach and view it as a must win situation. They will become forceful and domineering focusing totally on their own needs and ignoring the needs of others. They may become entrenched in their position and will not be willing to listen to others. In extreme circumstances they may escalate from frustration to aggression and even violence (both verbal and physical). They see all conflict situations as only having a win/lose outcome and try to overpower others with their words and actions. They may become defensive and dismissive if they feel they are not winning and/or the other person is gaining the upper hand. When dealing with subordinates they may become autocratic, using rank and authority to put an end to the conflict. They will have a strong tendency to tell others exactly what their opinion is and not listen to information or facts they do not agree with.

The D Style of Management:

When in a management position the D's style of communication tends to be direct, factual, and bottom line focused. As discussed previously they tend to avoid wasting time on small talk or social niceties and this may cause them to be perceived as blunt, cold, or uncaring. When delegating tasks to others they tend to spend so much time on the required result that others may have difficulty finding out just how to do it, and if they fail to deliver the D will not only tell them but also show them exactly how to do it. The D style person may have difficulty delegating authority or letting go of the responsibility because they want to maintain control of the situation. They tend to tell people what to do in a forceful and direct manner and will always focus on the results. They may be so forceful and direct that people have a difficulty in raising questions and/or clarifying their understanding. Staff reporting to a D style manager may be reluctant to point out issues or problems as they fear the response of the D's behaviour.

When developing people they tend to believe that the hands-on approach is the best way to learn, they try to force people to be self starting and self-directed and can become impatient with having to provide detailed instructions. They want routine reports to be short and concise, only wanting detail if there is an issue or problem to be solved. Their focus on results may cause them to overlook the contribution of staff members towards achieving a result. Reward and recognition may only be given when the goal is achieved, if the goal is not achieved the contribution will be ignored and the D will choose to focus on why the result was not achieved. Their perceived lack of concern for others well-being may cause staff members to withhold personal information when dealing with sensitive issues.

nature of their ideas and/or actions. Acknowledge their ability to get the maximum results with a minimum investment of time and effort. When providing praise, make sure you acknowledge the result and focus on their specific achievements and/or input to achieving the result.

How to provide feedback:

If the D style person is not achieving the results focus the feedback and discussion on the obstacles they are facing and what is stopping them achieving the results they require, help them focus on how they can eliminate these barriers to success. Discuss the desired changes in their behaviour in terms of potential impact on achieving results. Describe any current negative consequences from their behaviour and request solutions from them. Make sure your feedback is factual, neutral and non-judgemental. Help reduce their defensiveness by focusing solely on actions and consequences. Do not enter into right/wrong debates or win/lose situations as this will take the focus away from the desired changes required. Keep the feedback discussion focused on actions rather than emotions or intentions.

In a conflict situation:

The D style person will take a direct, aggressive approach, resulting in an "*I win, you lose*" outcome, therefore it is important to acknowledge their logic or reasoning by saying "*I can see your point*" or "*I can see the logic in your argument*". After acknowledging their inputs calmly restate your point. Avoid focusing on who is right or wrong by acknowledging the differences between the two of you, without judgement. You may need to accept that the only workable, win-win solution may be to agree to disagree. Counter any blaming statements by refocusing on the issue and what corrective action is going to be taken. Resist any impulse to retaliate with blaming, attacking or sarcastic comments. Reduce your own defensiveness when attacked and acknowledge any error on your part. Try to use open ended questions to define the real issue in the situation. Get them to focus on solutions by asking them what it is that they want as an outcome. Be prepared to call a timeout if emotions escalate to high levels of aggression or hostility, but make sure you schedule a time to continue the discussion. Always finish the discussion with a summary of what each person has committed to do to resolve the conflict.

When engaged in problem-solving/decision-making:

Due to a D's tendency to take practical, results orientated approaches to implement immediate solutions you may need to help direct them towards considering the long-term consequences of their decisions. They may need coaching on handling complex problems due to their natural tendency to oversimplify in a rush for immediate results. It may be helpful to encourage the D style person to take enough time to gather sufficient information and consider possible consequences before making decisions. Ensure you point out the benefits of taking more time in terms of the potential improved results.

When managing a D:

When you want to focus on developing someone with a D style behaviour help them get productive quickly. Show them the simplest, quickest, most practical way to get results. Emphasise the key details necessary to get the desired results. Make sure you define clearly the limits of their authority and control. Provide motivation by giving them opportunities to work independently and allow them to direct the efforts of others where possible. Offer them options for achieving goals, provide challenges and opportunities to win.

When complimenting someone with the D style use brief, direct statements, focusing on achievements, results, and their leadership abilities. When counselling them focus on obstacles to achieving the results and how they can eliminate them. Present needed changes in terms of impact on results and consequences. Ask them for solutions, do not provide them unless they cannot provide an alternative.

When delegating to a D style tell them what results you need and by when, let them determine how it will be done where possible. Specify clearly the limits of authority and available resources, allowing authority within those stated limits. Make sure they clearly understand what is expected of them and make sure you point out any behavioural expectations around how they should achieve or complete the task. Emphasise the level of control they have over resources that are required to complete the task. Where possible give them full control over the resources they require.

When you need to correct a D style person be firm and direct, specifying the desired result as well as the current level of performance. Make sure you direct the discussion to what they are going to do to eliminate the gap in performance.

Remember to keep your communications direct and to the point and try to focus conversations on the achievement of goals and their potential impact or consequences. When asking a D to report, be aware that they are demotivated by routine reporting and/or detailed information that they feel is not required. Agree a process of how and when they need to report and specifically what the report must and must not contain.

To help a person with a D style increase their effectiveness try to raise their awareness around the impact of their behaviours and help them understand how they can improve results by:

- taking more time to think through possible consequences before taking action
- listening and considering the input, feelings and experiences of others
- learning to negotiate outcomes on a win-win basis
- explaining their reasoning process rather than just announcing their conclusions
- learning to participate in a group or team without being in charge
- developing tact and diplomacy in communications and interactions with others
- giving recognition to others for their efforts and inputs.

This concludes the introduction to the person with a D style on the DISC map. Later in this book we will explore additional strategies for successfully dealing with and/or managing a person with a D style and its associated behaviours, for now let us look at the I-style or an Influence style from the DISC map.

Chapter Three: Introducing the I-Style

Influence– Fast-Paced & People Focused.

3

Introducing the I-Style

With a fast pace and a focus on people, the high I delivers on results and achieves goals through their Influence and motivational style and behaviour.

The second behaviour factor of the DISC model we will look at is that of the I for influence behaviour style. Located in the top right of the disc map the I style behaviour is fast-paced and people orientated. As with the previous chapter we will focus on a pure style of I for influence, later in this book we will explore the blended styles associated with the I for influence behaviour. Now let's have an introduction to the I behavioural style by looking at their associated strengths, weaknesses, behavioural traits, and examples of how they behave in certain situations, such as in conflict, when influencing, in communications, and when managing or being managed.

An Introduction to the I Style:

People with the behavioural traits of an I style may be generally described by the following attributes:

- optimistic
- motivated by praise
- socially and verbally aggressive
- can see the big picture
- people orientated.

People with a high I style often attempt to influence others through motivation, talking, engagement, and activity. They also tend to be more emotional and open in their communication style. A person with a high I style will often tell you more than you want to know. High I people can be described as trusting, self promoting, emotional, impulsive, persuasive, gregarious, and enthusiastic. The high I style will tend to attempt to shape the environment by persuading and influencing others. They enjoy involvement with people and making a favourable impression. They are motivated by social recognition, group activities, and developing relationships. They have a fear of social rejection, disapproval, and loss of influence. People with a high I style are very enthusiastic, charming and sociable. This style can also cause them to be quite impulsive, disorganised, and they may lack follow-through. When observing the high I style you will notice enthusiasm and engagement across a broad range of interests. The high I style enjoys being the centre of attention and is constantly looking for recognition for their contribution. They may become demotivated and/or sulky if this praise and recognition is not provided on a regular basis. Other styles may see this as overly needy. The high I style thrives when working with people and they lose interest when isolated for long periods of time.

In the workplace the I style can bring the following strengths to a team or group:

- they make themselves available to others
- they like to inspire others
- they can spread their enthusiasm and positive attitude
- they can provide positive feedback to co-workers.

On the downside they may come across as disorganised and/or lacking in focus. Some may see their behaviours as superficial and fluffy. When working on projects they may be more motivated by the initial start and lose interest with the details and lack follow-through.

How to recognise the I style:

The I style will appear highly extroverted with a focus towards people. They tend to be more indirect and may appear disorganised. Although they have good intentions they may not be great at setting goals unless they are held accountable in doing so. In a conflict situation they tend to try and use humour to defuse the situation. They are geared towards having fun with people and enjoying the experience.

A Typical I in the Workplace:

The high I tends to be very sociable, entertaining and emotionally expressive. They tend to be highly spontaneous; they generally prefer a relaxed and informal atmosphere. The high I style tends to be quite popular and enthusiastic, enjoys being the centre of attention and makes new friends quickly and easily. They openly trust people straightaway and initially may be very accepting of others regardless of their background, position, appearance or personal style. They have a tendency to openly express this acceptance both verbally and non-verbally. The high I will attempt to avoid purposely antagonising anyone as they are motivated by being socially accepted. They like to seek a favourable work environment in which they can continue to develop and maintain good relationships with their co-workers.

The high I will always seek approval and recognition, they enjoyed being popular. As they enjoy being the centre of attention they may seek approval from a small group of people who are important to them, however, they tend to cultivate a wide range of friendships and relationships ranging across various work and social circles. They enjoy being with people and may spend little time on solitary activities. The high I enjoys stopping for a chat inviting others into their office or workspace for discussions. If there is a social event on, the high I will be there as it is an opportunity to be with people. They also thrive on meetings, committees, and at conferences as they get to engage directly with a wide range of different people.

Hi I styles tend to be verbally articulate and are extremely good at promoting their own ideas and creating enthusiasm for the projects of others. Through their wide circle of friends and acquaintances they will personally promote the credibility of friends and colleagues and their work.

By utilising their strong social skills people with a high I behavioural style will often relieve tension in a group or reduce the discomfort that often exists when people meet for the first time. They will typically use humour and entertainment to reduce stress, in such a situation the high I person finds it easy to approach new people as they are very accepting of others and freely expressive in appreciation of others. Their primary goal in doing this is reciprocation as not only do they like, but also need the social interaction and positive appreciation for themselves.

People with a high I style are usually very optimistic, however, they may misjudge the merits of the situation or the abilities of others due to this overly optimistic view. From time to time they may jump to favourable conclusions without considering all the information or facts. Since they tend to highly regard the ability of people to express themselves in words, they may accept a well worded statement as valid without any further investigation. On the flipside they may have difficulty relating to or understanding a person who doesn't say much or their verbal skills are limited.

As the I person tends to be drawn to people or activities involving interactions with others they may be less interested in task accomplishment. They may even have difficulty controlling and planning their own time. They may be late for appointments and fail to meet deadlines unless they work closely on managing their time. When under pressure they may become even less organised and/or less careful.

The high I person will regularly over use compliments and appreciation, especially when feeling pressured. They have a tendency to become sentimental and overly emotional in difficult situations. The high I will make promises and provide praise in an effort to gain acceptance from others. This may lead the high I to over committing and under delivering.

Their approach to problem-solving or decision-making is very innovative. High I people tend to be very open to new ideas, they actively solicit suggestions from others. There is a risk however that they are likely to base a decision on feelings rather than on facts and they may be reluctant to properly investigate a situation and/or look for the detailed data. The trial and error approach is common among high I people, they will try all different possible solutions that come to mind until they find one that works.

What an I Wants:

The I style person is motivated by working in situations where they can provide positive feedback to others and engage in positive interactions. They enjoy opportunities to verbalise their thoughts and feelings. They work best in environments where two-way dialogue is encouraged and appreciated. They actively seek out psychological strokes and enjoy enthusiastic verbal recognition such as *'great, fantastic, brilliant'* or *'we could not have done this without you'*. The high I person wants to have their feelings and emotions acknowledged and appreciates immediate positive verbal feedback. The high I person wants to work within an environment which is fast-moving and involves relating to others with enthusiasm. They want opportunities to be creative, imaginative, and engage in brainstorming.

They typically like to avoid situations where others may react to them with hostility or dislike. They do not want to have to choose between being liked and being respected. They may be demotivated when having to focus on follow through or extensive details. They try to avoid routine, repetitive tasks. They do not work well in environments with rigid time constraints and/or little or no contact with other people.

How an I Likes to do Things:

In this section we will look at how the I style person prefers to do things such as: how they like to communicate, how they like to make decisions, how they manage their time, their approach to problem-solving, how they deal with stress, and how they approach conflict situations.

Communications

The I style likes to communicate frequently in person or on the phone in an informal, friendly manner, covering a wide range of subjects. They tend to be spontaneous and fast-paced, and very expressive with their emotions and feelings. They feel comfortable with people who respond to their emotional expressions and they are most at comfort in expressing positive emotions and using words such as *'great'*, *'fantastic'*, and *'brilliant'*. The high I likes to talk about their enthusiastic, optimistic plans and dreams. They may feel rejected by and/or uncomfortable with people who are more reserved in their expressions, both verbally and non-verbally.

They find it quite difficult when communicating negative information directly to people as they are worried about how it might impact the relationship or how they are viewed by the person. This may cause other people to be unclear or confused as to the real issue or the seriousness of the problem because of the lack of directness. They find it difficult being tough when situations require a direct or assertive approach as they may attempt to smooth over situations or cajole people who are arguing, without addressing the real issues.

They may have many discussions with people but fail to follow up on the actions discussed due to their tendency to over commit and under deliver. They find it hard to say no to requests as they do not want to upset the other person or damage the relationship.

The high I wants to approach all areas of interaction where possible with face-to-face communications, wanting to talk about everything and they may not be sensitive to other people's preferences in communicating, assuming that everyone likes to talk. They may behave in a way that other more reserved people find intrusive. The high I will have a tendency to be overly expressive in all communications including email, notes, letters, and most of all, in person or by phone.

Decision-making

The high I tends to use an emotional approach to decisions basing them on gut feelings and intuition. They have a tendency to be overly optimistic in expectations of other people and situations and sometimes can neglect to seek out all the facts and information. They may respond impulsively and not take enough time to gather the required data. When making decisions they may regularly expect the best, failing to consider possible negative consequences. They may avoid making decisions which involve interpersonal conflict, losing approval or looking bad. The high I person does not like to make decisions that require them to choose between people as they will be worried about how the other people may view them after the decision is made.

Time management

The I style tends to prefer open ended structures with flexible schedules; they do not like to work in a strict time constrained environment. A lot of the time they will spend more energy and focus dealing with the people and the processes than on the tasks. They may have difficulty limiting time spent with people, getting behind schedule and completing activities. Due to this fact they may be chronically late for appointments.

Due to their approach to time management the high I can leave others feeling frustrated and angry at their perceived lack of time management as they provide less structure and predictability then is comfortable for others. They may want to keep time more loosely structured and fail to commit to a schedule, which may not meet others' planning needs.

Problem-solving

The I style behaviour will typically tackle all problem-solving situations with the same approach, they want to involve others in the problem-solving process and enjoy bouncing ideas off people or brainstorming to find a solution. A collaborative approach to problem-solving is one that they tend to favour. They will also approach problem-solving on a personal, emotional basis and can become impatient with a more methodical approach. Similar to their decision-making processes they like to go with instinct and gut feeling. Although the I is quite capable of solving problems on their own they will automatically want to involve others, sometimes delaying potential quick action with a need to engage others.

Stress

The high I style may have a tendency to ignore stress and/or try to avoid it by seeking new opportunities to enjoy life and have fun. This can lead them to experience stress from too much of a good thing, as they may be over using avoidance tactics. Usually they are quite able to forget about negative situations in the past, focusing on positive expectations for the future. When a past event involves a strong emotional situation where they were impacted negatively this may not be as easy to forget or let go. A lot of the time the high I will reduce the build-up of stress by becoming emotionally expressive and letting off steam.

They will find environments of chronic hostility and pessimism very stressful and will do their best to avoid such situations or environments. One of the tactics they use to reduce stress is that of interacting with others, trying to laugh, talk, and attend social events. The high I finds appreciation and affection from others to be very effective in reducing the stress levels. As a result of their approach to stress management they may become worn out from too many social commitments, especially during holidays or when interacting with close personal friends.

Conflict

In a conflict situation the I style will take a collaborative approach trying to smooth over the conflict by use of communication and/or humour. Where possible they will try to avoid or completely ignore conflict as they are worried about the effect it will have on their personal relationships. Sometimes they will try to resolve conflict indirectly through engaging with others to try and resolve the conflict and avoiding direct interaction. If the high I views the conflict as a personal attack they may become defensive, withdrawn, and sulky.

The I Style of Management:

When in a management position the I's style of communication tends to be frequently in person or on the phone in an informal, friendly manner, mixing personal talk with business discussions. They tend to be spontaneous and emotionally expressive. They can have difficulty in communicating negative information directly, leaving other people confused as to what the real issue may be or the seriousness of the problem. A high I style behaviour finds it extremely difficult to criticise performance or to provide negative feedback and as a result staff members reporting to an I style manager can be unaware of performance issues. Although they can have many discussions with people they may fail to complete written documentation or to follow up on a regular basis.

The I style manager likes to delegate tasks that require attention to detail and follow through (since they tend to avoid these activities themselves) but due to the fact that they only give general information this can lead to misunderstanding in terms of who is responsible or what is expected. They also have a tendency to overestimate other people's ability and/or understanding of a task/situation and this can lead to a lack of completion of the task. They tend to be optimistic in their expectations of others and may need to spend more time finding out about actual skills as they may fail to check back on progress of delegated work.

When directing people they will focus on verbal inspiration, always emphasising the positive. They have a tendency to become too friendly and too involved with some people and due to the close relationship may have difficulty being tough when situations require a direct or assertive approach. They may attempt to cajole or indirectly influence people who are resisting or arguing.

They tend to present the big picture with enthusiasm and positive expectations and they may overestimate someone's ability and fail to provide sufficient, specific direction where required. They tend to offer a lot of verbal encouragement and provide positive feedback, praise, reward and recognition.

They tend to use an emotional approach to decisions and problem-solving, basing them on gut feelings and intuition. They have a tendency to be overly optimistic in expectations of people and situations. They may avoid making decisions which involve interpersonal conflict or losing approval.

When trying to motivate others they tend to use positive and enthusiastic language and provide public recognition and praise choosing to downplay the negative and avoid constructive feedback.

How to deal with an I:

If you find yourself working with somebody who has an I style of behaviours, here are some tips for creating a positive relationship:

Creating a positive climate:

Where possible show an interest in them by asking personal questions and providing opportunities to interact with others in a positive, enthusiastic manner. Allow time for discussions where they can verbalise thoughts, feelings and ideas. Accept that they tend not to pay attention to details in relation to tasks and offer assistance to them by helping them follow-up on specific details. Listen responsively to them and show appreciation for their efforts. Accept that they prefer to avoid negative or unpleasant discussions and try to keep your communications positive where possible. Note that they will have a desire to interact often and with many different people.

Communicating with an I:

Try to utilise the informal approach using open ended discussions in social environments such as over lunch or dinner. Provide them with an opportunity to share experiences, stories and ideas in an enthusiastic, responsive exchange. You may need to direct them to stay closer to the subject under discussion in order to finish within a reasonable timeframe and be aware that they will have difficulty listening to negative information.

How to provide recognition:

Use enthusiastic public praise for their verbal ability and interpersonal skills. Compliment them on positive changes in their appearance, specifically noting any significant change in their dress or in the way they present themselves. Acknowledge and welcome their persistently optimistic attitude in situations that you might find discouraging. Recognise their skill at involving others in discussions and activities. Acknowledge their ability to motivate others even in difficult situations. Make sure you compliment their ability to organise social functions and praise their ability to generate enthusiasm in others.

How to provide feedback:

When providing feedback to a high I give them the opportunity to express their feelings after hearing your feedback. Acknowledge these feelings and direct the discussion to facts and results, resist their attempt at sidestepping the discussion, redirecting their attention to the situation in hand. Use open ended questions (who, what, where, when, how) to keep the discussion focused. Discuss specific action plans for change rather than general statements about changes in attitude or behaviours. Remember to validate their work as a person separate from the desired changes in their behaviour. Counter any emotional escalation by focusing on specific actions and behaviours and showing them the positive outcome of these new actions and behaviours. Always invite them to restate your feedback in their own words to ensure accurate listening. Close the discussion with a specific statement of what actions they are going to take as a result of your feedback.

In a conflict situation:

The I style person will take an indirect approach to conflict preferring to avoid open, direct conflict. Make sure you always acknowledge their discomfort around dealing with conflict by saying something like '*I understand this may be uncomfortable for you*', and then presenting the details to them. Try to state the issue factually, without judgement about them as a person as they will have a tendency to take negative feedback personally. Allow them to verbalise their feelings. Respond to their feelings by saying '*I understand you were angry (sad, cross, glad, scared)*'. Try to limit sidetracking in the discussion by acknowledging other issues that may need to be discussed at another time, and immediately move back to the current issue being discussed.

State repeatedly that this conflict is about a specific issue and not about them personally as high I people tend to fear loss of approval. Counter their attempts to minimise the problem by focusing them on actions and consequences to themselves and others. Also counter their attempts to placate you without solving the problem, by requiring a commitment from them around specific actions. Try to direct the discussion to the specific facts and actions rather than talking in generalities or emotional expressions. Close the discussion with a clear statement of what is going to happen and by when, try to affirm the value of the discussion in maintaining a positive relationship with them.

When engaged in problem-solving/decision-making:

As a high I tends to avoid handling complex, detailed problems requiring follow-up they may need to be coached through a logical problem solving process instead of relying on their gut feelings. Be aware that they may have difficulty acknowledging that a problem exists due to their optimistic perception of the situation. You may need to explain the actual or potential consequences of the problem to them clearly. To help them fully understand the situation show them the impact on people. Remember that they try to avoid making decisions involving negative consequences and/or interpersonal conflict, so discuss with them how to make such decisions while minimising the negative consequences or potential conflict. Finally discuss how making the decision or solving the problem will reduce the negative outcomes in the long-term. If needed explain how indecisiveness will frustrate others and make them look bad.

When managing an I:

When you want to focus on developing someone with an I style behaviour use a fast-paced, enthusiastic approach to the development. Get them involved quickly in new situations where they can begin building relationships and trust. Try to reduce the amount of details to avoid overwhelming them initially and provide a safe environment for them to ask questions. Always check understanding by requesting specific feedback on how-to do the task. A great suggestion is when they agree to a goal ask them how they are going to achieve it, try to focus on the specific behaviours. Always provide assistance in developing structure for completing tasks.

When trying to motivate someone with a high I style behaviour make sure you provide opportunities for them to interact with others in a positive, enthusiastic manner. Always allow time for discussions where they can verbalise thoughts, feelings and ideas. Provide assistance in following up on details and provide opportunities for visibility and recognition.

When you want to provide compliments to a person with a high I style make sure you use enthusiastic public praise for their verbal ability, and their interpersonal skills. Remember they will have an ongoing need for positive reinforcement and psychological strokes. A safe bet is that you can never over praise a high I. Even in situations where the task is not successfully completed try to acknowledge and appreciate their efforts and inputs.

When trying to counsel a high I provide opportunities for them to express their feelings, acknowledge these feelings and direct attention to the facts and results. Try to use open ended questions to generate specific action plans for change. Switch to closed questions when you need them to focus on actions.

Try to provide help and direction to a high I when working on problem-solving or decision-making by offering help on complex and detailed problems that require follow-up. Coach them through a logical problem solving process and help them avoid relying on gut feeling and instincts. If they have difficulty acknowledging a situation or problem focus on the potential consequences to the people involved.

When delegating to a high I style person make sure you clarify understanding and gain acceptance of specific performance expectations and the timeframe for completion. Make sure they fully understand the consequences of not delivering within the agreed expectations. Make sure you establish dates for process checkpoints with clear understanding of what needs to be completed and by when. Allow the high I person to express their feelings and emotions related to the task you are delegating. Provide help in structuring the process for completing the tasks, especially when dealing with complexity or assignments requiring a methodical approach. At the end of the delegation session ask the high I to repeat back the expectations to check for clarity.

If a high I style person becomes overly expressive or emotional in the workplace this may be an indication that they are not receiving the appreciation and approval they require. Try to identify specific behaviours and acknowledge the positive intention of these behaviours.

Be aware that when a high I has to work in a conflict situation they will tend to use avoiding tactics and/or humour to diffuse the situation. You may need to provide coaching to help them understand the impact of their behaviours in a given situation. The high I can sometimes act or say things without thinking first, allow them a safe environment in which to apologise and rebuild any damage done to relationships. If you need to correct a high I's behaviour be aware that they will try to sidestep the problem or downplay the importance. Resist these attempts at sidestepping the problem by stating the performance problem and consequences very specifically and clearly. Try to direct the discussion towards how they will specifically improve performance, avoiding extensive discussions about other people and other situations. Always end the discussion with a compliment or comment about their enthusiastic approach and try to gain commitment about when and how they will achieve the desired outcome. If required, focus on the positive outcomes of improving their performance and looking good in the eyes of others.

Always remember that the high I style behaviour prefers informal, open ended discussions in a more social environment, such as over lunch or dinner. Always try to communicate with them face-to-face or at least over the phone and avoid the use of e-mail, memos, or letters. Remember that they desire an opportunity to share their experiences, stories and ideas in an enthusiastic response of exchange, so encourage this when communicating with them. When communicating note they will need to be directed to stay closer to the subject under discussion in order to finish within a reasonable timeframe. Remember they will have difficulty listening to negative information so you need to focus on the positive and raise awareness about the impact of specific behaviours and how it may be letting others down or making them look bad.

Always remember to check and determine whether the seriousness of the discussion was understood and acknowledged. Above all, when managing a high I provide them with an environment where they can be innovative, creative, and provide motivation and encouragement to others. Where possible avoid assigning tasks that require them to work in isolation as they prefer to engage with others when working.

To help a person with an I style increase their effectiveness try to raise their awareness around the impact of their behaviours and help them understand how they can improve results by:

- developing a more realistic assessment of people and situations that includes negative and positive information
- structuring a process for completing tasks in an orderly and timely manner
- developing the ability to be firm and direct when dealing with interpersonal conflict
- willingness to hear and consider negative thoughts and feelings of others
- following through on key details on a more consistent basis
- better management of time requirements
- evaluating the amount of time spent in meetings and verbal communications with others.

This concludes the introduction to the person with an I style on the DISC map. Later in this book will explore additional strategies for successfully dealing with and/or managing a person with an I style and its associated behaviours, for now let us look at the S-style or a Steadiness style from the DISC map.

Chapter Four: Introducing the S-Style

Steadiness– Steady Paced & People Focused.

4

Introducing the S-Style

With a steady pace and a focus on people, the high S delivers on results and achieves goals through their interpersonal skills and consistent style and behaviour.

The next behaviour factor of the DISC model we will look at is that of the S for steadiness behaviour style. Located in the bottom right of the disc map the S style behaviour is steady-paced and people orientated. As with the previous chapters we will focus on a pure style of S for steadiness, later in this book we will explore the blended styles associated with the S for steadiness behaviour. Now let's look at the S style and their associated strengths, weaknesses, behavioural traits, and examples of how they behave in certain situations, such as in conflict, when influencing, in communications, and when managing or being managed.

An Introduction to the S Style:

People with the behavioural traits of an S style may be generally described by the following attributes:

- loyalty to those they identify with
- a very good listener
- extremely patient
- orientated towards family activities
- motivated towards traditional procedures.

People with a high S style often exhibit behaviours such as displaying a preference for a steady pace, security, and avoidance of sudden changes. High S people are described as possessive, sincere, team orientated, predictable, loyal, patient, and passive. Their orientation towards a steady pace and people focus makes them very dependable. They like an environment where they can achieve stability and accomplish tasks through cooperating with others. They have a tendency to be calm, patient, loyal, and are good listeners. They are motivated by infrequent change, stability, sincere appreciation, and cooperation. Their main fears are a loss of stability, the unknown, change, and unpredictability. When engaging with a high S person you will notice patience, their ability to be a team player, a methodical approach to problems, an avoidance of conflict, a calm approach, and the willingness to put other people's needs first. Due to their quiet nature and intolerance of conflict others may see the high S as indecisive, indirect, or somebody who resists change. The high S can unfortunately be seen as a pushover and may be exploited by other behaviour styles such as the high D or high I style. The high S style person may also come across as unable to make decisions, but this is due to the fact that they do not want to cause disharmony and or make decisions that may affect other people.

In the workplace the S style can bring the following strengths to a team or group:

- they are a good team player
- they are sensitive to other's needs
- they approach meeting agendas methodically
- they are excellent listeners
- they are extremely likeable to others.

On the downside they may come across as indecisive and weak. Due to their passive nature others may see them as a pushover and they could be open to being bullied in certain situations. As they like to work at a consistent pace within a consistent environment they may also seem resistant to change.

How to recognise the S style:

The S style can appear highly introverted with a focus towards people. They may be indirect in their approach to situations and can sometimes be overly possessive. They tend to set short term and low-risk style goals and they are geared towards trust and harmony. Their typical response to conflict is to tolerate and/or avoid/ignore.

A Typical S in the Workplace:

A typical S style person tends to be fairly low-key and easy-going. They tend to take a moderate stand on most issues. They generally prefer to think through an issue before taking any action. Although they may try a new approach that has been carefully tested, they may prefer to use methods that have worked well in the past, avoiding risky, untried approaches. The S style person may prefer to cooperate with others to obtain the results they desire and generally tends to work well with most people. They are very considerate, patient, and willing to help those they consider friends. They will regularly build close relationships within a relatively small group of friends. The S style person will usually be available for extra work, provided it does not infringe too greatly on family or personal time.

The high S style person prefers to keep things as they are, they are most comfortable and effective in a steady and predictable environment. The S style person likes to develop regular work routines, together with well-planned methods for getting results. They may tend to focus on consistent performance and are capable of performing routine activities for an extended period of time. As a result, they generally tend to achieve a remarkably consistent level of performance over time.

The S style person is a very effective and good listener. They will try to accommodate the wishes of others, and may often compromise their own needs to meet the needs of others. They will also compromise to avoid conflict, and easily adjust to a wide range of personal styles. They tend to bring increased harmony to any given situation. The high S is very much a team player; they may evaluate others based upon friendship, as well as, performance and competency. The high S will tolerate others behaviour to avoid conflict.

The high S often tends to be an excellent short-term planner. Once they understand what is expected and the resources that are available to them they will carefully plan and organise their work to ensure an acceptable outcome within the established timeframe. The S style person will always tend to get the job done by working consistently over a period of time.

As a high S tends to view modesty as a desirable trait they may be reluctant to talk about their accomplishments and bring them to the attention of others. They may see this as bragging which is a behaviour they are not comfortable with in themselves or in others. As a result, their skills and talents may not be fully utilised or appreciated by others.

The high S may need some help in getting started on new projects and they may be less likely to initiate a new activity on their own. They may also need some help getting a project completed as they may tend to put aside work which is essentially complete for later finalisation. They may also need some help in developing shortcut methods and procedures for meeting deadlines. In a project management situation they will avoid any conflict situations and will tend to take on additional work themselves to avoid upsetting or frustrating others.

Since change typically happens in all organisations and this may disrupt the consistency of their performance the high S style person may be slow to adapt to change. In fact, when faced with sudden, unplanned change, they may become somewhat stubborn. However, when given advance notice and adequate time to prepare, they can be a real asset in the process of implementing change. They need to fully understand the reason for change and the benefits it will provide. Without this they will be reluctant to get engaged with the change process.

The high S may tend to have some fear of disorganisation and instability. Such conditions may interfere with their consistency of performance and may make their coping skills less effective. This may have a demoralising effect on them as they fear the loss of stability and harmony. Depending on the abruptness of the changes or the amount of pressure they feel the high S will intensify their efforts to restore the status quo. For a while, they appear not to be coping well with the changes. Before long, however, the natural tendency is to adapt and accommodate to the wishes of others may reappear. The high S can soon begin to regroup their inner resources, assess the new situation, and develop new coping skills to deal with it effectively. Soon they may have developed a new status quo which they will work to maintain.

Although they rarely tend to hold a grudge, a high S person may be unlikely to express their negative feelings such as anger. Consequently, this unexpressed anger may build up and perhaps then unexpectedly erupt, when the pressure becomes too great.

When approaching a problem or decision the high S style person may prefer to rely on established practices. When this is not possible, they generally tend to be open to suggestions from others. They carefully consider all the facts and every alternative, thinking about the matter for some time before coming to a conclusion. The greater the potential risk, the more time they require to make their decision.

If the high S person finds themselves in a conflict situation or rapid changing environment for too long they will start to seek permission for everything they do, even the little things. This is driven by the desire to not increase the conflict and/or disharmony.

What an S Wants:

The S style person is motivated by situations where they can work cooperatively with others in a positive team environment. They enjoy providing needed support to others through products and services, for example they make excellent customer service agents. They like to have clearly defined areas of responsibility and authority. They like to maintain a predictable, orderly work environment where changes are kept to a minimum. They like to work within a harmonious, informal, friendly work environment where there is time for interpersonal discussions about family and friends. They also enjoy working in an environment where loyalty is rewarded with job security.

When working the high S style person wants predictable tasks and activities, these need to be provided to them with clear instructions and expectations. They desire a working environment with little or no interpersonal hostility or conflict. They like to take methodical approaches to completing their work and enjoy applying tried and trusted methods. Above all they have a need for their co-workers to be friendly, informal, and cooperative.

They want to avoid situations with high levels of unpredictability and uncertainty. They are discouraged by disorganised and disorderly environments, they will become uncomfortable in situations where other people may become hostile and/or aggressive. They do not like ambiguous situations with uncertain outcomes or situations where they are required to become aggressive. They do not want to have to provide a solution without having the time to study the situation thoroughly first. They also require support and encouragement from their manager. They dislike working in a competitive environment as in their opinion this leads to interpersonal hostility and conflict.

How an S Likes to do Things:

In this section we will look at how the S style person prefers to do things such as; how they like to communicate, how they like to make decisions, how they manage their time, their approach to problem-solving, how they deal with stress, and how they approach conflict situations.

Communications

The S style person prefers to communicate through the use of an informal, low-key, friendly approach to others. They have a desire to talk with others and a willingness to listen patiently to the thoughts and feelings of others. They like to involve others in discussions of how things are going in their lives, demonstrating a genuine interest by nodding approval, smiling and asking questions to solicit additional information. The high S style person will tend to communicate on a regular and predictable basis preferring to have face-to-face communications in a friendly manner.

The high S style person is more comfortable with a moderate use of emotions and expressions rather than an intense use of emotions and expressions. Others may underestimate the intensity of their feelings due to this more reserved approach to expression of feelings and emotions. The high S style person is slow to express anger, they may internalise their feelings and experience physical stress due to bottling up their emotions over time.

The S style behaviour will avoid interpersonal conflict, so they may have difficulty in expressing their thoughts and feelings in some situations, especially when they feel a conflict or difficult situation may escalate. As they desire security they may have difficulty communicating in what they perceive to be a high-risk situation.

They will be very uncomfortable when communicating with hostile or aggressive people and may feel frustrated and resentful at their own failure to speak their mind.

Decision-making

The S style approach to decision-making tends to be extremely factual, and they like taking the time to think things through, considering the impact on others and the long-term stability and security of the group. The high S style behaviour may procrastinate on decisions involving interpersonal conflict or involving changes that involve risk taking. They may solicit advice from others in complex situations, or situations outside their own area of expertise. They will regularly consider past experiences and use these to evaluate current situations and guide them in decision-making. They like to involve others in the decision-making process if they are going to be affected by the decision.

Time management

The S style person prefers to work in a predictable and regular routine by applying an established schedule. They like to work with a specific plan for how things are going to be done, including a to-do list. The S style person may become bogged down in routine procedures, losing the flexibility to respond to changing situations. They may become overwhelmed with commitments of their time, due to a desire to help others. The high S style person has difficulty in saying no to others, particularly if they become angry or show disapproval with them. They may become overloaded because they also have a difficulty asking others for help. The high S style person will regularly work additional hours to complete scheduled tasks on time to avoid upsetting others. They may spend a lot of time procrastinating over decisions and worry too much about the outcomes and impact on other people.

Problem-solving

The S style likes to converse with others when trying to solve problems, using a deliberate, methodical approach. They have a tendency to prefer solutions that are low risk and have proven successful in the past. They are strong supporters of the tried and trusted method and may have difficulty adapting to new problem-solving techniques. They will also find difficulty when dealing with complex problems, requiring innovative solutions which may involve high risk and/or impact to people. Due to their approach to problem-solving others may find their adherence to traditional practices very frustrating.

Stress

The high S style person will tend to seek a slower paced, more relaxed approach to life, finding time for friends and family as well as for work. They may find rapid change and unpredictability very stressful, causing much anxiety and exhaustion. The high S style person may also have a tendency to become quiet and non-expressive when stressful changes are occurring, working diligently to restore some order to their life. They may also become worn out and overextended because of their inability to decline other people's request for help. The high S has a tendency to avoid confronting conflict and/or uncomfortable situations and will allow distress to build over time, even to the point where physical illness may result.

The high S style person prefers to relax by spending time at home, working on hobbies, or with family or friends. Another source of stress relief can be working on routine projects that have standardised processes and procedures that produce results. They may also be comforted by the support and understanding of fellow work colleagues.

Conflict

The high S style person will try to avoid conflict at all costs preferring to seek harmony in situations. They will always try to avoid interpersonal aggression and will seek to find solutions that are acceptable to everyone. They also have a tendency to ignore issues while trying to restore harmony hoping that the problem will go away. In a conflict situation they may attempt to calm agitated people through open discussion and effective listening. When faced with a conflict you will notice the high S style person become more quiet and reserved. They may also feel powerless to do anything about the conflict. If the conflict situation persists over time the high S style may choose to remove themselves from the work situation as they see this as the only way to avoid the conflict.

It is important to note that due to their perception the high S style person may see a situation as hostile when others do not. For example a person with a high D style behaviour who is simply pushing for results and putting pressure on for outcomes will not see their behaviour as hostile or creating conflict, whereas the high S style may find this behaviour quite uncomfortable and deem the situation to be both hostile and a source of conflict.

The S Style of Management:

When in a management position the S's style of communication tends to be informal, friendly, open and honest. They like to create a friendly approach and will demonstrate a willingness to listen. The high S likes to involve the team in discussions of how things will be done. They will present information in a methodical, step-by-step approach, asking for feedback at regular intervals. They may have difficulty communicating with hostile or aggressive people. They may often have a tendency not to provide constructive feedback as they are concerned this may create hostility.

When the S style manager wants to delegate they tend to prefer to develop a methodical, planned approach to assigning work to others. They like hands-on involvement with the work, so they may have difficulty delegating work with which they feel both comfortable and confident completing themselves. They tend to follow through by checking back on a regular basis and by being available for help. The high S style manager prefers to delegate work to people who are cooperative, non-argumentative, and perform consistently. They may correct other peoples work after the fact rather than confront someone in case they become hostile. They will provide a lot of information in a clear and precise manner when delegating to others. Sometimes they may provide a range of options so as to not push too hard with the individual by forcing them to do it in one specific way.

When directing people the high S style manager prefers to give specific assignments with clearly defined processes and procedures. They have a tendency to follow up on a regular basis and like to have scheduled feedback sessions with employees to check on progress. They may have a difficulty being assertive with hostile or aggressive people when trying to hold them accountable for performance.

When developing other people the S style manager prefers to show people how to do things in a step-by-step manner and will use a structured approach to training where ever possible. They will provide regular feedback and respond to questions with patience and understanding. People who have a different, quicker style of learning may become frustrated by this methodical approach to training.

The high S style manager will tend to motivate others by building relationships of trust, predictability, and rewarding loyalty. They will try to promote the benefits of teamwork and cooperation at all times.

Their approach to decision-making and problem-solving tends to be factual using deliberate, methodical approaches. They will tend to avoid situations that may become hostile or generate conflict within the group. Sometimes they will employ slower methods or unnecessarily detailed processes just to avoid conflict.

As a high S manager their style and approach to time management is a preference to operate within a predictable routine with established schedules, they will have a tendency to expect this from others also. They will encourage people to use to-do lists and to report regularly on status updates.

How to deal with an S:

If you find yourself working with somebody who has S style of behaviours here are some tips for creating a positive relationship:

Creating a positive climate:

Where possible always acknowledge how their efforts are helpful to you and to others. Schedule predictable, regular activities in which they can participate. Provide opportunities to cooperate with others in achieving results. When suggesting change, layout a step-by-step plan showing the reasons for change and the benefits of change. Initiate low risk discussions with them to express their thoughts and feelings. Accept that they have a tendency to avoid confrontation and that they may be uncomfortable in hostile situations. Be aware that they prefer familiarity and predictability to variety. Always display your appreciation warmly and openly towards them.

Communicating with an S:

As a high S tends to be somewhat reserved they may not initiate discussions in some areas, be aware of this and plan for how you will tackle such situations. Provide regular opportunities for informal and casual discussions. Be aware that the high S prefers to receive new information in a logical manner, with enough time to ask questions. Note that they may not spontaneously talk about concerns, worries and conflicts that they may have with other people. Provide opportunities for drawing out their concerns in a low risk setting. When communicating with a high S style person allow them time to discuss family and friends in a warm and comfortable environment. Allow extra time for them to reflect on questions before asking them for an answer.

How to provide recognition:

Always use warm and sincere statements showing the value of their efforts and maintaining stability. Compliment their ability to build and maintain harmonious, cooperative work relationships and their effectiveness as a listener. Acknowledge how their ability to consistently produce concrete results is important to you and to others on the team. Try to identify specific behaviours that contribute towards the success of the organisation in general. Praise their continuing concern for meeting the needs of others and providing help and support to colleagues. Always acknowledge their efforts at building team loyalty and involvement, reward their ability to help the team work together in a harmonious setting.

How to provide feedback:

When you want to provide feedback (both positive and negative) to a high S style person remember to provide feedback on specific behaviours in a low-key, informal, non-aggressive manner. Take time to draw out their thoughts and feelings about the current situation. Balance the discussion of what changes are necessary with an acknowledgement of what areas in which their actions can contribute positively to the relationship. Assist them in developing a step-by-step plan for change if requested or required. Discuss a reasonable timeline for changes acknowledging any concerns that they may have. Provide encouragement and support for developing a set of behaviours in situations that they may find stressful or uncomfortable. Acknowledge that the change may result in some stress in the short-term but focus on the reasons for change and the long-term benefits. Emphasise the importance of harmony and cooperation that will result from these changes. Acknowledge their value and work as a person, separate to the desired changes. Always offer the opportunity for follow-up on any feedback provided.

In a conflict situation:

As a high S tends to avoid conflict or hostility, especially in an interpersonal setting try to acknowledge their discomfort by saying *'I realise you're uncomfortable with this'* or *'it is important we resolve this so we can return to harmony'*. Always state the need to have this discussion in order to maintain the familiarity and stability of the work environment. Make sure you describe the issue without any judgement or blame. Try to solicit their thoughts and feelings about the issue, recognising that they may be somewhat reserved in their expression of feelings and emotions.

Draw out issues that they may be uncomfortable with by asking open ended questions (how, what, where, when, who). Ask them what they would need to resolve the issue in a way that is reasonable and effective. Ask them what they would see as a win-win solution for everyone involved in the conflict. Try to counter any potential tendency for them to give in just to maintain harmony, without resolving the conflict, by creating a low risk opportunity for them to discuss what they would really like to do if maintaining harmony was not an issue. Address their concerns about how this conflict may affect the security of the relationships or situation by stating, factually, what the logical consequences may be, if any. Try to affirm their work as a person and continued value to the group. Close the discussion with a clear statement of expectations, outcomes and consequences, reaffirming the importance of the discussion in maintaining the harmony and stability of the work environment.

In a constant changing environment or where hostility and/or conflict is persistent try to identify situations to allow the high S style person to disengage from this type of environment. Look for ways they can contribute without dealing directly with the difficult situation they find uncomfortable.

When engaged in problem-solving/decision-making:

Due to the S's style of problem-solving or decision-making it is important that you try to provide the following to assist them in making decisions and solving problems. Encourage them to use step-by-step, methodical approaches to solving problems and allow them to rely on proven processes and procedures. Where this is not possible help them explore alternative situations and/or options that will produce the results they require while minimising the impact on people. Be ready to offer assistance in developing innovative solutions to problems in new areas. Remember that they tend to prefer having time to study problems before implementing solutions so give them time to think. Be aware that they may need direction in determining when situations require study and which require immediate action.

Always allow them time to think through things in a step-by-step manner and support their methodical, logical approach to some decisions. Discuss which decisions may be lower risk and perhaps can be made more quickly while still achieving the desired outcome. As they may tend to procrastinate on decisions involving interpersonal conflict be available to offer support and coaching in this area. Always discuss how decisions will improve harmony and stability within the work environment.

When managing an S:

When you want to focus on developing someone with an S style create a step-by-step plan for the development and provide one-to-one or hands-on instructions. Make sure you have written procedures wherever possible and allow more time for them to become comfortable and/or to feel confident with a task. Provide regular feedback, and friendly follow-up and reassurance. Allow them time to ask questions and provide answers that help them understand the importance of the development and how it will contribute to the harmony of the group.

To motivate a high S demonstrate how their efforts are helping others and recognise and reward their consistent and predictable performance. Make sure you provide opportunities to work cooperatively with others to achieve tangible outcomes. Reward their loyalty and support to the team and acknowledge their excellent listening skills.

To compliment somebody with a high S style behaviour use warm, sincere statements about the value of their efforts and maintaining stability, building harmonious, cooperative relationships, and producing results consistently.

If you are required to provide counselling to somebody with high S style behaviour make sure you take time to draw out their thoughts and feelings about current situations. Help develop a step-by-step plan for change with a defined timeline and identify the importance of the change and the positive impacts it will produce. Provide encouragement and support for developing assertive behaviours. Acknowledge that the change may be stressful to them in the short-term, emphasising the benefits to everyone once stability has been restored. Always try to focus on the positive impact to the larger group and how they can help support this.

When delegating to someone with high S style behaviour provide a step-by-step explanation of what is required, with written documentation where possible. Be available for regular follow-up and to handle any questions they may have. Clarify which resources are available for completing the assignment and how they can access these resources. Provide assistance in gaining cooperation from others when necessary.

Provide support and coaching with problem solving and decision making, especially in the area of interpersonal conflict or hostility. Encourage and help them to use different methods for new situations and/or challenges. Where possible allow them time to study problems before implementing solutions. If they have a tendency to procrastinate on decisions show them how this may affect the group's effectiveness and that it could impact on harmony.

If you need to correct a person with high S style behaviour make sure you balance statements of what improvement is necessary with acknowledgements of the areas in which they are performing well. Provide assistance in creating a step-by-step plan for improvement and encourage them to ask questions. Provide regular positive feedback for incremental improvements and show them how this is positively impacting the organisation and/or the group. Make sure you separate issues of performance from issues of worth as a person.

When communicating with a high S style behaviour be aware they may be somewhat reserved and tend not to initiate discussions. Provide regular opportunities for informal, casual discussions where they can focus on friends and family. When presenting to them remember they like information in a logical manner and they like to be given enough time to ask questions. Note they may not spontaneously talk about concerns, worries and conflicts with other people. Provide opportunities to draw these out.

To help a person with an S style increase their effectiveness try to raise their awareness around the impact of their behaviours and help them understand how they can improve results by:

- developing the ability to respond to unpredictable change
- learning techniques to be more assertive with people in given situations
- initiating discussions to resolve ambiguous situations and/or to deal with conflict
- stretching towards new challenges
- increasing their flexibility in their work routines and how they approach situations
- looking for possible shortcuts to make their work routines more efficient
- dealing with conflict as it arises instead of letting it build over time
- expressing their emotions more openly to others when they are upset or frustrated
- saying no, rejecting additional work requests when already overloaded.

This concludes the introduction to the person with an S style on the DISC map. Later in this book will explore additional strategies for successfully dealing with and/or managing a person with a S style and its associated behaviours, for now let us look at the C-style or conscientiousness style from the DISC map.

The Steadiness style is a loyal and committed team player.

Chapter Five: Introducing the C-Style
Conscientiousness– Steady Paced & Task Focused.

5

Introducing the C-Style

With a steady pace and a focus on task, the high C delivers on results and achieves goals through their precision and meticulous consistent detailed style of behaviour.

The next behaviour factor of the DISC model we will look at is that of the C for conscientiousness behaviour style. Located in the bottom left of the disc map the C style behaviour is steady-paced and task focused. As with the previous chapters we will focus on a pure style of C for conscientiousness, later in this book we will explore the blended styles associated with the C style behaviour. Now let's look at the C style and their associated strengths, weaknesses, behavioural traits, and examples of how they behave in certain situations, such as in conflict, when influencing, in communications, and when managing or being managed.

An Introduction to the C Style:

People with the behavioural traits of a C style may be generally described by the following attributes:

- critical thinkers
- work towards and expect high standards
- extremely well disciplined
- accurate and precise
- motivated by the right way to proceed.

People with a high C style often exhibit behaviours such as adhering to rules, regulations, structure, and seeking to do quality work and doing it right the first time. A person with a high C style can be described as courteous, conventional, systematic, diplomatic, accurate, and analytic. They will tend to want to work within situations where quality and accuracy are rewarded. They perform tasks with an excellent attention to standards and details, and provide excellent analytical thinking during problem solving and decision making situations. They like to have clearly defined performance expectations where quality and accuracy is highly valued. They dislike criticism of their work and/or people taking shortcuts that may impact on quality. The high C style has a tendency to be overly critical of self and others; they find it quite easy to provide negative feedback and sometimes may come across as stubborn and a complainer. The high C style likes to analyse information and data and due to this preference they have a tendency towards indecision as they like to have all the information well-documented and reviewed before they decide on the correct action to take. With a preference for a steady pace and task focus the high C may have difficulty working with other DISC styles who do not have the same approach to quality and accuracy. The high C works well in a controlled environment where rules and regulations need to be adhered to.

In the workplace the C style can bring the following strengths to a team or group:

- they are thorough
- they want to follow standards
- they like to emphasise accuracy
- they will use diplomacy when dealing with people.

On the downside they may come across as overly concerned with perfection, and expect others to perform to the same high standards as themselves. Due to their behaviour style some may say they act aloof. They may tend to hamper others' creativity by sticking to the rules rigidly.

How to recognise the C style:

The C style will appear highly introverted with a focus on tasks. They tend to be direct when dealing with issues and problems and sometimes have a tendency to be overly critical. They are very good at setting safe goals that have been tried and tested. They enjoy developing procedures and analysing information. They have a tendency to avoid conflict and may be uncomfortable in change situations unless the need for the change is clearly documented and understood.

A Typical C in the Workplace:

A typical C style person tends to be meticulous, calculating and precise in most everything they do. They have a tendency to be quite logical, having the ability to examine a situation analytically and to base their conclusions and actions on the facts and information without any emotional interference. As the high C style behaviour has a desire to avoid appearing incompetent, they typically engage in lengthy, careful preparation before undertaking any project or activity in order to ensure success. They strive to master skills privately before using them in front of others. In fact, they may be likely to exercise caution in most situations. They tend to relate their sense of self-worth to the quality of their efforts and performance. To this end a high C will be likely to demand high quality not only in their own performance but the performance of work colleagues.

The high C style has a desire to avoid antagonism or hostility from others, because of this they may suppress or deny their own aggressive tendencies. They may seek to maintain a peaceful environment, free of any interpersonal conflicts and as a result they may appear to be very diplomatic and non-aggressive. Despite this mild appearance, however, the high C may have a strong need to control their environment. One way in which they can exert this control is by requiring adherence to mutually accepted rules and regulations. They will also use standards to dictate and control the performance of others. If this is not enough to achieve control they may resort to indirect forms of control. This can include carefully developing a plan to obtain the results they desire by controlling the conditions of the work environment. They will typically also gather as much information as possible to support their position, using the facts to override any arguments put forward by others.

One of the key strengths of the high C style behaviour is their natural tendency to be analytical. However, they may have a tendency to over use this ability. They may over use analysis in an effort to avoid being wrong, particularly when they bear sole responsibility for a decision or an activity they are involved in. They can also over use analysis if they are facing a new or uncertain situation. This can cause them to temporarily lose sight of the 'big picture' and find themselves bogged down in details.

In pressure situations the high C can be somewhat of a worrier, they may hold things up unnecessarily, seeking an unrealistic level of certainty or perfection before they proceed. This can cause frustration and annoyance to others and also cause trouble for the high C themselves.

As the high C tends to value their own analytical abilities they also judge others by this standard. They enjoy learning, fact-finding, and seeking out new information so they can present logical arguments. They will also find considerable satisfaction in reasoning and analytical activities. They have a tendency to hold individuals who have high credibility and track records in high esteem. They may respect those who think before they act and collect the adequate information before making any decisions. On the other hand, they may have much less tolerance for those who are highly emotional, impulsive, or lack their level of analytical skills. They also dislike people who are emotional in their decision-making or aggressive with their interactions toward others.

The high C enjoys being valued as part of a team or workgroup, however, when it comes to getting things done, they generally prefer to function on their own, as they can control the situation and work towards standards to ensure that they get it right first time.

What a C Wants:

The C style person is motivated by situations where they can perform to their own standards and expectations. They enjoy having control over those factors that affect the quality of their performance. They will thrive in an environment where quality and accuracy are highly sought after and rewarded. The C style person enjoys being 'right' and wants to be in a position where they can present facts and information to support their arguments.

The high C style person wants to work within an environment which provides a plan or system for performance which provides specific detailed feedback. They want a reserved business-like atmosphere where people are task orientated and professional. When given a task or project they want to have enough time to complete tasks to their own standards. When taking on a new task or project the high C style behaviour demands that the expectations are clearly defined and the information required is either provided or they have a source to acquire this information.

Based on their behavioural styles the high C wants to avoid situations that are ambiguous, undefined, or emotionally heated. They want to avoid situations in which their performance may be criticised and/or where they are being held accountable for the quality outcomes in situations where they have insufficient control over the task or other people's performance. They do not want to be put in a position where they have to defend inferior performance and/or quality in products or services. They dislike being put in a situation where they are required to respond to others without time to evaluate the possible consequences and/or situations that require personal disclosure. The high C will be extremely demotivated when rules or expectations constantly change without justification or explanation.

How a C Likes to do Things:

In this section we will look at how the C style person prefers to do things such as; how they like to communicate, how they like to make decisions, how they manage their time, their approach to problem-solving, how they deal with stress, and how they approach conflict situations.

Communications

The C style person prefers to communicate through the use of formal and diplomatic approaches when dealing with people. They have a tendency to be reserved, precise and detached when communicating with people they do not know well. The C style behaviour will use logic and data to persuade others rather than using any emotional appeals. They enjoy using formal, written communication, documents and discussions in situations where there has been a misunderstanding or conflict in the past. They have a preference for a reserved, impersonal, business-like approach in communications when dealing with people other than their close work colleagues. Due to this communication style they may be perceived by others as cold, detached and uninvolved due to their lack of verbal and non-verbal expression and emotion. The high C style behaviour will have a tendency to be uncomfortable with other people's emotional displays, preferring to remain detached and restrained in their own expression.

They may be more comfortable in expressing negative emotions such as anger, displeasure, disappointment, and criticism rather than positive emotions. They tend to be uncomfortable expressing these positive emotions verbally such as joy, affection, happiness, and desire. They may prefer to write a note or letter to more completely express their sentiments. The high C style behaviour is typically slow to trust, or to reveal personal information until the other person has proven their trustworthiness.

The high C style person will have a preference to have one or two close, long-term friends as confidants, and they can be quite verbal and expressive with these close friends. They have a tendency to be sarcastic in their expressions, using a sometimes scathingly dry wit. They enjoy debating facts and information in situations where they are comfortable, they are always ready to use logic to win an argument.

Decision-making

The C style approach to decision-making tends to be extremely factual and careful, they like to gather information and assess any possible risk before making decisions. They want to postpone risky decision-making until they have all the information or defer these decisions to others or at least get an expert opinion. They are at risk of getting stuck in information gathering and analysis mode due to their fear of making the wrong decision. They are prone to paralysis by analysis in their decision-making and dislike 'what if' scenarios. Be aware that the high C style behaviour may experience high levels of aggression and self-criticism over past decisions that did not lead to the desired outcomes and/or achieve their high standards. They will have a tendency to review past experiences to find a more perfect, failsafe process for making decisions.

Time management

The C style person prefers to follow a systematic approach, taking pride in finding unique, efficient techniques that produce high-quality results. They may be critical of others who do not use such a systematic approach. They tend to have high standards and may spend more time gathering information and perfecting results than is justified. They may have a difficulty managing time due to their professionalism.

They may have difficulty delegating to others because no one else can meet their level of high standards. They may need to develop new standards for their performance that are more appropriate to current conditions and the demands on their time. The high C style person will typically spend more time designing and developing a time management plan than actually focusing on managing their time effectively. They will have a tendency to re-do documentation over and over until they are satisfied it is 100% accurate.

Problem-solving

The C style person tends to use an analytical approach to solving problems, considering many variables in developing potential solutions. They may be very effective in solving complex problems but may spend far too much time analysing the simple problems. They like to use *Information Systems* to anticipate problems and to analyse situations. They always try to develop the perfect solution and may lose sight of other realities such as deadlines or human impact.

Stress

The high C style person may experience moderate to high levels of stress as a result of them trying to meet their own high standards on a continuous basis. Since they are driven to achieve perfection this may result in a chronic state of frustration with themselves and others. They are constantly worried about adequately preparing for the future, spending time thinking through contingency plans and possibilities. The high C style behaviour perceives the world as a somewhat hostile environment, requiring constant vigilance on their part to ensure that things go correctly. They need a certain amount of private time to relax and process their thoughts and feelings about the events of their lives. They may become somewhat hostile and critical when overloaded, being driven by an inner inability to rest until everything is done right. The high C style person may have difficulty shutting down their internal critic in order to get some rest as they are constantly analysing their own performance and the performance of others.

Conflict

The high C style person may not deal very effectively with conflict; initially they may withdraw from any situations where conflict is present so they can plan a strategy for response. They will tend to try and avoid any situations where conflict may arise. When they are faced with conflict they may become very defensive and attempt to overpower others with facts and logic. They may use indirect aggression and/or passive resistance choosing to nod and agree but not act in certain situations. This passive aggressive type behaviour will cause them to appear to comply but fail to follow through. They may become rigid and unbending and become more entrenched in their own position. When in a conflict situation they may withhold information and reduce their level of communication. In extreme situations they may become aggressive if their personal values or beliefs are under threat.

The C Style of Management:

When in a management position the C's style of communication tends to be systematic using logic and data to persuade others. They have a tendency to use formal, written communication, documenting discussions with others and staff. They prefer a reserved, impersonal, business-like approach in oral communications. As a manager they try to avoid discussions involving personal information or highly emotional situations. They tend to avoid socialising in the work environment preferring to keep relationships on a business level. They may be perceived by others as cold, detached, and uninvolved due to this style of communication. The C style manager may overload staff with information, facts and figures, and details.

When delegating the C style manager tends to give specific, detailed instructions for all assignments. They may be reluctant to delegate certain types of work preferring to do the important work themselves so that they can be sure it will be done correctly. They may have difficulty finding people who meet their high standards and may not delegate to individuals who have not proven themselves. After delegating tasks the C style manager will typically monitor progress and results so closely that others may feel under pressure and inspection constantly. The high C style manager prefers working with people who share their high standards and commitment to quality performance.

When a high C style manager is directing people they have a tendency to be impersonal, precise, and factual. They focus on what needs to be done, how it is done, why, by whom, and when. They may prefer to give assignments in written, formal communications, requesting specific feedback in response. They may also have a tendency to over control the work of others checking on quality by frequently questioning people. They have difficulty with people who resist close supervision.

When a high C style manager wants to develop people they have a preference for a systematic, comprehensive approach to training, with competency requirements specified and assessed. They will set high standards for performance and may become critical, impatient, and demanding of others if these high standards are not constantly achieved. Due to their behavioural style they believe in ongoing training and skills development to this end they will constantly provide resources to staff members for their development.

As a high C style manager tends to be a careful decision maker they may spend a lot of time gathering in information and assessing possible risks before making decisions. They may want to defer risky decisions to higher levels of authority or at least get approval before making decisions or taking action.

With their strong focus on accuracy high C style managers may set extremely high standards and spend far too much time gathering information and perfecting results to meet the standards than is justified. As they want to use a systematic approach to time management themselves they may become critical of others who do not use such an approach.

When the C style manager is in the problem-solving mode they will use an analytical approach, considering many variables in developing any potential solutions. Although they may be very effective in solving complex problems they may spend far too much time analysing simple issues. As they always want to develop the perfect solution they may lose sight of other realities such as deadlines and the needs of others.

When motivating others the C style manager will provide specific information on what is expected and provide feedback on performance, stating the logical benefits and impact.

How to deal with a C:

If you find yourself working with somebody who has a C style of behaviours here are some tips for creating a positive relationship:

Creating a positive climate:

When trying to create a positive environment for a person with high C style behaviour try to create opportunities for them to demonstrate their knowledge and expertise and always validate their efforts at achieving results that meet their high standards. Try to provide situations where their logic and systematic efforts will contribute to the long-term success of goals and/or the organisation. Accept that they may be reluctant to express their feelings and provide them with opportunities for private time. Be aware that they may be quiet and observant in most social situations and do not force them into emotional situations and/or conflict. Try to provide opportunities for them to talk knowledgeably with others about a specific subject. Accept they need to be 'right' and their distress at mistakes, especially if they are their own.

Communicating with a C:

As a high C tends to prefer communication to be somewhat formal in new situations try to avoid personal references and/or discussions until a solid relationship has been created. Understand that they tend to be matter-of-fact, preferring a logical presentation of information rather than any emotional expressions. Be aware that they may have difficulty storing information that is in conflict with their perception of how things should be done. Always check for points of disagreement or misunderstanding and give them time to ask questions and/or explain their point of view. Allow them to aggressively question the information presented in an effort to reconcile any conflicting sources of information.

Always respond to their questions with specific information in a non-defensive manner. As the high C style person likes to analyse information, provide them with time to process new information before requesting a response.

How to provide recognition:

When you want to compliment somebody who has a high C style make sure you use concise, accurate, specific statements, preferably in private. Make sure you compliment their competence in a specific skill area and relate how their actions have achieved the desired results. Praise their continued commitment to meeting their extremely high standards and compliment their tactful, discreet or subtle approach to difficult situations. Acknowledge their ability to remain calm and detached in emotionally charged situations. Provide recognition for the value of their insightful thinking in complex situations. Validate their use of logic in handling problems.

How to provide feedback:

When providing feedback to a high C style person try to take time to reduce their potential defensiveness by acknowledging their areas of competence first. Always list specific behaviours and the consequences of those behaviours, both positive and negative. Remember to keep the discussion factual, accurate, logical, and impersonal. Specify any needed change, explaining why the change is necessary and the importance of the change. Make sure you solicit their thoughts about the solution and/or situation. Try to provide them with an opportunity to think about the situation before requesting them to respond. Let them develop a strategy for change before committing to a specific course of action. Avoid right/wrong type discussions.

In a conflict situation:

As a high C style person may initially withdraw from open conflict you need to provide an environment where they have time to reflect and think about a specific situation. Be aware that the high C style person can become aggressive when their personal value system or standards are under attack. Try to state the issue calmly, logically, factually, citing specific behaviours and/or situations. You may want to try to reduce their defensiveness by acknowledging their thoughts, without reacting defensively, by saying something like '*I can see your point*' or '*that's interesting please tell me more about that*'. Listen to their thoughts, and then redirect the discussion to the current issue. Try to minimise the time spent discussing all the factors contributing to the issue in the past by focusing on what is going to be done right now to resolve the conflict.

Counter any statement of blame or attack by acknowledging that you heard what they said, and, without discussing it, move back to the issue under discussion. Counter any critical statements about your behaviour by acknowledging that your behaviour may have been less than perfect, without becoming defensive. Try to explore what they need to do to resolve this conflict on a win-win basis. Allow them to take some time to think about the conflict situation before they respond. Always affirm that your intent is to resolve the conflict, not to criticise or attack them personally. Counter their tendency to use passive resistance as a form of indirect aggression by asking them to state specifically what they intend to do and when. Establish clearly what you both understand to be the next steps in the situation to resolve the conflict. Always state that you value their full, insightful approach to the situation and their desire to resolve the issue on a reasonable, equitable basis. Suggest that you schedule a time in the future to review the situation more formally, with more depth, and allowing them time to prepare their thoughts.

When engaged in problem-solving/decision-making:

Remember that the high C style tends to prefer an analytical, systematic approach to solving problems, considering all contributing factors and possible consequences. Be aware that they may need to be coached on alternative problem-solving techniques for problems that need more immediate solutions. Remember that they tend to want to find the perfect solution and where appropriate, you will need to encourage them to spend less time analysing and perfecting, instead focusing on the action to resolve the problem or make the decision. Understand that they need help in developing a workable solution rather than a perfect solution. Since their approach to decision-making is an analytical one where they like to calculate the risks and potential payoffs, try to provide them with the benefits for making quick decisions. Understand that they may want more time to gather information and/or test their assumptions. Discuss what are appropriate amounts of time to spend in the analysis phase and assist them in setting a time limit for when the decision is due. Be aware that they can get bogged down in details especially when dealing with 'what if' concerns. Finally remember that they may need reassurances on what the personal consequences of being wrong will be.

When managing a C:

When you want to focus on developing someone with a C style make sure you demonstrate in a logical manner, explaining the rationale for each procedure that you are trying to initiate. Always check understanding at key points with the high C style person ensuring that they fully understand and agree with your requests. Make sure you provide time for them to process the information and practice the skills on their own. It is important that you allow them to develop a competency in private before expecting them to perform these skills in public. Be available to respond to any questions and provide additional explanations and information. Make sure you define time limits for developing the adequate skill rather than perfecting mastery.

When motivating a person with a high C style behaviour make sure you create opportunities for them to demonstrate their expertise. Support their efforts at creating quality results. Try to provide situations where logical and systematic efforts will contribute to the long-term success of the goal and/or organisation.

When you want to provide recognition and reward to a high C style person make sure you focus on the specific skills and/or tasks, providing detailed information on what they did and how it had a positive impact. Use concise, accurate, specific statements (preferably in private) about their competence, use of logic, efficiency, and precision.

In situations where you are required to counsel someone with high C style behaviour take time to reduce potential defensiveness by acknowledging their area of competence first. Specify any needed change, explaining why the changes are necessary and solicit their thoughts about the situation. Provide them with the opportunity to think about the situation.

Allow them time to think about potential solutions and to develop a strategy before committing to a specific course of action.

Due to their analytical approach they may need to be coached on alternative problem-solving techniques for problems that need a more immediate solution. They will want to be analytical and systematic in their approach to solving problems and allow the time to consider all contributing factors where possible. Be aware that they want to find the perfect solution and provide help in developing a functional solution rather than a perfect one.

When you are delegating to someone with a high C style behaviour provide logical, accurate, concise descriptions of the performance expectations, including standards for quality and the desired outcomes. Explain why the assignment is being done and how it is necessary to the overall performance of the organisation. Make sure you provide opportunities to discuss alternative ways of completing the assignment, determining what resources are available.

Be aware that if you need to correct someone with high C style behaviour they will have a tendency to become defensive when their own performance is criticised. Stick to a specific, factual discussion of what the current results are and what performance is required. Allow them time to create and record a plan for improving their performance or correcting any mistakes. Close any discussions by clarifying and getting agreement on what the improvement will be and by when. Set a date to formally review any progress. Try to counter-act any defensiveness by focusing on factual information and helping them understand how they can improve their performance.

When you want someone with high C style behaviour to make a decision understand that they will want time to gather information. This is due to their approach to decision-making being analytical, calculating, and detailed. They will want to review all the information, weighing up all potential factors and calculating the risk and/or potential payoffs before making any decisions. Try to discuss appropriate amounts of time to spend in the analysis phase and make sure you set a deadline for when the decision is due. Try to avoid giving them 'what if' scenarios or situations as they may become bogged down due to the lack of detail and/or information. Provide them with reassurances of what the personal consequences of being wrong will be.

Remember that the high C style prefers communication to be formal and business-like, avoiding personal references and discussions. Always state the purpose for the communication upfront, covering the topics in a logical, systematic order. Where possible provide advance notice of any meetings and/or discussions to allow them time to prepare. They may have difficulty storing information that conflicts with their perception of how things should be done so make sure you check for points of disagreement or misunderstanding. Do not get defensive if they aggressively question the information you are providing, this is their way of analysing information. Make sure you respond to all of their questions with specific information and try to adopt a non-defensive manner. Provide them with time to process any new information before you require them to respond. Try to set a time to meet and finalise any discussions and/or communications that are not concluded within the allotted time or where they need to reflect on the information before providing a response.

To help a person with a C style increase their effectiveness try to raise their awareness around the impact of their behaviours and help them understand how they can improve results by:

- Balancing their adherence to high standards with their attention to deadlines
- responding non-defensively to comments about their performance
- modifying criticism of others work by considering feelings as well as facts
- sharing knowledge and information with others in a non-condescending manner
- practising self-disclosure and appropriate expression of feelings
- developing a willingness to negotiate performance standards
- becoming more open to other people's systems for doing things
- avoiding rigidity in their thinking and their need for being right.

This concludes the introduction to the person with a C style on the DISC map. Now that we have covered the four basic dimensions of the DISC map in D-I-S-C we shall look at identifying the relationship between each style. The next chapter will look at the behaviour style of people with multiple factors within their style, such as the D-I style, or S-C style etc.

The high C style of behaviour is task focused and steady paced.

Chapter Six: Discovering Your Style

No one is just a D-I-S- or C, we are a blend of styles.

6

Discovering Your Style

Less than 2% of the population are 'pure-styles' consisting of just a D with no I, S, or C, or just an I with no D, S, or C, etc. We are a blend of all four styles.

Now that you have a good understanding of the four basic styles or factors that make up the DISC model it is time to explore what is known as the blended styles. Less than 2% of the population are high in only one style while low in the other three. A much more common profile is that of a person high in 1-2 styles, and medium to low in the other styles. For example: High D, Medium I, Low S and C, or High I and High S, Low D and Low C. It is however, uncommon to be high in 3-4 styles, typically a person will be high in no more than 2 styles and medium to low in the others. This is due to the dichotomy between the diagonal styles (D – S and I – C).

With the D-S dichotomy and the I-C dichotomy both the pace (fast versus steady) and focus (task versus people) are opposite, therefore it is very unusual to find a person that naturally displays behaviours on both sides of this dichotomy on a continuous basis.

We are all capable of displaying the behaviours associated with each style of the DISC model depending on the specific situation we are faced with and/or the mindset/mood we find ourselves in when tackling a specific challenge. For example, Sam is usually a very steady person with a strong focus on building and maintaining relationships, a real natural S-style person. In the workplace Sam typically likes to work in teams, helping other members and providing encouragement and support when people are not at their best. Sam also avoids conflict, preferring to let things 'blow over' instead of confronting them face-to-face. However, Sam has very strong personal values and beliefs around the use of manipulation tactics. If Sam feels someone is trying to manipulate another member in the team/group Sam will be VERY direct and verbal about the situation, Sam will speak very aggressively with a raised voice and clearly state what is and is not acceptable. These are typical behaviours associated with the D-style of the DISC model (which is the polar opposite of Sam's natural style). Also Sam is a very keen sports fan and can quote all of the statistics and facts related to the national soccer team for the past 50 years and is quick to correct anyone who may state a fact or statistic that is incorrect. Again this may seem more like the behaviours of a C-style person, but as we know Sam is a natural S-style.

Depending on the specific situation, and/or our personal beliefs and values people may respond differently to their natural style. It is important to look for continuous behavioural indicators to identify their natural style.

A good indicator to a person's natural style on the DISC model can be assessed over time and across different situations. When trying to diagnose someone's specific style look at their behaviours over different situations and ask yourself are they more task or people focused, and are they more fast or steady paced? Below is a quick diagnostic tool to help you identify a person's style. Remember to look at the behaviours over time and across a range of situations for a more continuous pattern:

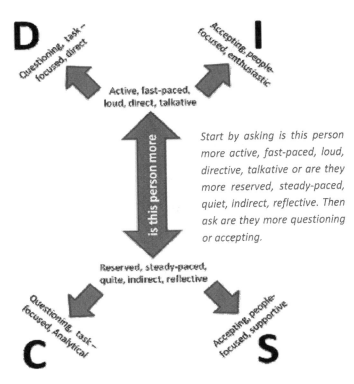

Start by asking is this person more active, fast-paced, loud, directive, talkative or are they more reserved, steady-paced, quiet, indirect, reflective. Then ask are they more questioning or accepting.

As a quick indicator you can also ask yourself what is this person usually like when under pressure or in a conflict situation? Psychology will show us that people 'revert to norm' or 'return to type' in these situations.

Due to the dichotomies it is very unusual to observe a person with a natural style of D-S, S-D, I-C, or C-I. However, these styles may be seen when a person is under extreme stress or reacting to continuous exposure to an environment where their basic needs are not being met. We will discuss how to deal with these behaviours in a later chapter, for now let's look at the common blended styles associated with the DISC model of behaviours:

The D-C Style:

With a common focus on task the DC style can be described as a person with a focus on challenge, results and accuracy. People with the DC style prioritise challenge, so they want to explore all options and make sure that the best possible methods are used. As a result, they may be very questioning and skeptical of other people's ideas and motives. Since the DC person tends to be more focused on using their influence and energy towards achieving goals other people may not relate well to their challenging nature.

The DC person also likes to prioritise results, so they often come across as very direct and straightforward. They tend to focus on the bottom line and may overlook other people's feelings and emotions. Some people may describe them as quite blunt and insistent.

Another common trait of the DC style is their tendency to focus on accuracy. They enjoy controlling not only the situation but the quality of the work also. They have a preference to work independently where they are in full control of delivering the desired results. They like to achieve goals quickly and will tend to use a very systematic approach in their work behaviours.

Some Behavioural Indicators of the DC style:

Goals:	Independence, personal accomplishment, achievement.
Judges others by:	Competence, commonsense, ability.
Influences others by:	Determination, desire for results, high standards.
Overuses:	Bluntness, sarcastic or condescending attitude, aggression.
When under pressure:	Becomes overly critical, sarcastic, stubborn.
Fears:	Failure to achieve results and standards.

The D-I Style:

With a common focus on pace the DI style can be described as a person with a focus on quick action, new opportunities, and innovative results. People with the DI style have a tendency to prioritise action, and they may come across as adventurous and risk-taking. The DI style person has a tendency to grow bored easily, losing interest in activities quickly, therefore these individuals often seek out unique assignments and leadership positions. They are attracted to environments that are continuously changing. They like to keep things moving along and will typically work at a vigorous pace.

The DI person also likes to prioritise results and likes to accomplish their goals quickly. While they can be described as competitive, they can also use charm and influence to persuade others to help them succeed. They are quite talkative and like to take a lead position.

A person with the DI style will also value enthusiasm; they will come across as charming because of their high energy and engagement. They tend to use their excitement to inspire and motivate others towards the results they crave. They like to create a lively environment where they are seen as the centre of attention. They have a dynamic approach and can be seen as outgoing and very expressive.

Some Behavioural Indicators of the DI style:

Goals:	Quick action, new opportunities, innovative results.
Judges others by:	Level of confidence, ability to influence, engagement.
Influences others by:	Charm, risk-taking, enthusiasm.
Overuses:	Impatience, egotism, manipulation.
When under pressure:	Becomes aggressive, overpowers others, covert and manipulative.
Fears:	Loss of power, losing face, loss of status.

The I-D Style:

With a common focus on pace the ID style can be described as a person with a focus on action, enthusiasm, and results. People with the ID style have a tendency to prioritise action so they like to focus on moving towards their goals quickly. They have a desire to maintain a fast pace, and they are very comfortable making decisions quickly. They have an active and energetic pace and like to create momentum.

The ID style person also prioritises enthusiasm, with their high energy they like to rally others around a common goal.

They have a tendency to maintain a positive attitude and bring a genuine optimism to their work. They are extremely expressive and positive; they like to get excited about ideas.

With a focus on results the ID style also comes across as ambitious and goal orientated. They regularly enjoy using interpersonal relationships to achieve new accomplishments. They come across as highly driven and ambitious and will use influence and passion to bring others on board.

Some Behavioural Indicators of the ID style:

Goals:	Excitement, recognition, breakthroughs.
Judges others by:	Ability to think creatively, level of innovation, charisma.
Influences others by:	Risk-taking, enthusiasm, passion.
Overuses:	Impulsiveness, outspokenness, charm.
When under pressure:	Becomes impulsive, lashes out at others, sarcastic.
Fears:	Fixed/mundane environments, loss of approval or attention.

The I-S Style:

With a common focus on people the IS style can be described as a person with a focus on collaboration, enthusiasm, and support. People with the IS style like to prioritise collaboration. They enjoy working in teams and will look for opportunities to work with others as much as possible. They have a desire to help everyone feel included so they will spend time and energy trying to get people involved. They like to be perceived as the supportive leader of the group/team.

The IS person also likes to prioritise enthusiasm, so they often bring a positive attitude to the work they undertake and towards the relationships they build. They are motivational and encouraging, and they like to spread their optimistic spirit to other team members. They come across very upbeat and have a happy-go-lucky approach to solving problems and delivering results.

The IS person also values support, so they are extremely flexible people who want the best for everyone in the group. If other people are struggling they will show concern and offer uncritical support. They have a soft-hearted approach and sometimes this may affect their ability to deliver results as they may go easy on some people to avoid damaging relationships. If they have to make a choice between delivering a result and maintaining a relationship, they will prioritise the relationship.

Some Behavioural Indicators of the IS style:

Goals:	Friendship, support, recognition, appreciation.
Judges others by:	Ability to see good in others, warmth, openness, friendliness.
Influences others by:	Agreeableness, empathy, support, caring.
Overuses:	Patience with others, indirect approaches, avoidance.
When under pressure:	Takes criticism personally, avoids conflict, withdraws (fear of rejection).
Fears:	Pressuring others, being disliked, being rejected by others, and lack of appreciation.

The S-I Style:

With a common focus on people the SI style can be described as a person with a focus on collaboration, support, and enthusiasm. People with the SI style have a tendency to prioritise collaboration; they enjoy involving others in making decisions. They enjoy working with others and try to build team spirit and are less concerned with individual accomplishment.

The SI style person places a high importance on the needs of other people, so they also prioritise support. They have a very accommodating nature and will often put aside personal ambition to help meet the needs of the team. They strive for good relationships and place an emphasis on uncritical acceptance of other people's ideas and feelings.

The SI style person also values enthusiasm, they typically come across as very cheerful people. They tend to see the positive in most situations, and encourage other people's ideas.

Some Behavioural Indicators of the SI style:

Goals:	Acceptance, close relationships.
Judges others by:	Receptivity, empathy to others, approachability.
Influences others by:	Empathy, patients with others, support of other's needs.
Overuses:	Kindness, avoidance, personal connections.
When under pressure:	Avoid conflict, try to make everyone happy.
Fears:	Pressuring others, creating conflict and/or aggression.

The S-C Style:

With a common focus on pace the SC style can be described as a person with a focus on stability, support, and accuracy. People with the SC style place a high priority on stability and attaining consistent outcomes. They have a tendency to be cautious, preferring to work in a predictable environment that does not change or present a lot of surprises. They are not eager to take risks or act spontaneously; they prefer to apply safe, dependable methods.

The SC person also likes to prioritise support, they have a tendency to be accommodating and they are willing to forfeit their own needs and preferences when necessary. They are usually very patient and diplomatic; they are not likely to become overly emotional or expressive. They have a tendency to be cautious and avoid change situations where the rationale for change is not clear.

The SC style person places high value on accuracy. They like to work systematically to produce quality work and effective solutions. They have a tendency to be analytical and methodical, applying careful approaches to their work. In certain situations they may become inflexible when under pressure or working towards a deadline.

Some Behavioural Indicators of the SC style:

Goals:	Non-hostile environment, set objectives, steady progress.
Judges others by:	Reliability, rationale, realistic outlook, even temperament.
Influences others by:	Diplomacy, self-control, consistency, facts and figures.
Overuses:	Humility, analysis, willingness to let others lead.

When under pressure:	Becomes inflexible, hinders ideas and spontaneity, complies.
Fears:	Time pressure, uncertainty, chaos, rapid or sudden change.

The C-S Style:

With a common focus on pace the CS style can be described as a person with a focus on stability, accuracy, and support. People with the CS style can be described as orderly and precise. They prefer to be well prepared, structured and organised. They have a tendency to avoid taking risks or making rapid changes. They approach work with a cautious and methodical style. They enjoy presenting information on areas that they have expertise and knowledge.

The CS style person places a high priority on accuracy, they have a tendency to spend their time refining their ideas before presenting them and/or moving forward. They place a strong reliance on data and like to analyse all information before making decisions and tend to take an objective approach. Due to their careful and methodical approach they dislike being forced to make quick decisions.

Support is also highly valued by the CS style person and they are usually willing to help others when their expertise is needed. In the workplace they come across as even tempered with a patient approach to both people and difficult situations. They have a modest and obliging approach with a tendency to be less expressive and/or emotional. Due to their focus on support the CS style person will sometimes find it difficult to make decisions in situations where the right decision will have a significant impact on people. When faced with conflict their natural response is to withdraw and keep quiet.

Some Behavioural Indicators of the CS style:

Goals:	Stability, reliable outcomes, stable environment.
Judges others by:	High standards, orderly methods, thoughtfulness.
Influences others by:	Practicality, attention to detail, logic.
Overuses:	Traditional methods, sense of caution, facts and logic.
When under pressure:	Withdraws, gets bogged down, procrastinates.
Fears:	Emotionally charged situations, ambiguity, rapid change.

The C-D Style:

With a common focus on task the CD style can be described as a person with a focus on challenge, accuracy, and results. People with a CD style like to prioritise challenge and may come across as sceptical and determined. When presented with new ideas they will ask a lot of questions as they like to uncover problems that could affect results. They have a tendency to be overly critical and will question approaches and/or the ideas of other people. They may be seen as a barrier to new ideas and innovation.

With a high focus on accuracy the CD style person likes to focus on thinking logically and creating the best possible solutions. They tend to avoid letting their emotions get in the way of making rational decisions. They have a precise and analytical approach to situations and the tendency not to be overly expressive or rely on the use of emotions. The CD style person avoids putting '*Band-Aid*' fixes in place preferring to focus on implementing the correct solution.

As they also place a high value on results the CD style person will come across as extremely determined to deliver quality outcomes effectively and efficiently. They are comfortable taking charge of projects when necessary, and they can usually be counted on to keep things on track and within budget. They have a focus on bottom-line results and may come across as stubborn or demanding when these results are not being delivered.

Some Behavioural Indicators of the CD style:

Goals:	Efficient results, rational decisions, efficiency.
Judges others by:	Competence, use of logic, ability to deliver results.
Influences others by:	Strict standards, resolute approach.
Overuses:	Bluntness, critical attitude.
When under pressure:	Ignores people's feelings, moves ahead independently.
Fears:	Loss of control, failure to deliver results.

These are the eight common blended styles associated with the DISC model, in a later chapter we will explore some of the less common styles that may be observed when people are under extreme pressure or outside of the comfort zone for too long.

By now you should have a good indication of your own personal style on the DISC model, the information provided on the four generic styles and the eight blended styles will help you identify which factors are closely aligned with your behavioural tendencies.

If you are still unsure of which style best fits your behavioural type you can access additional information and resources through one of the many providers available online. These providers offer psychometric questionnaires to analyse your behaviours and identify your specific DISC behavioural style.

For a quick assessment of your own behavioural style take a look at the list of words below, and on each line select the word that best describes you and/or your behaviours. Try to select the word that is most like you, taking into account that it may not be exactly like you, but out of the list of options on that line it is the word that is **most** like you.

Ambitious	Expressive	Unassertive	Unsociable
Controlling	Playful	Too Trusting	Technical
Decisive	Whimsical	Supportive	Systematic
Demanding	Creative	Steady	Self Contained
Desire to win	Agitated	Indecisive	Rule driven
Determined	Idealistic	Seek Harmony	Risk Averse
Directing	Impulsive	Predictable	Quality Focus
Results Focus	Inconsistent	Modest	Precise
Get it done	Influential	Insecure	Picky
Pushy	Spirited	Empathic	Organised
Self Assured	Talkative	Easy going	Inflexible
Self Motivated	Unfocused	Dependable	Evaluative
Single -minded	Unsystematic	Accepting	Analytical
Domineering	Get Appreciated	Like to please	Get it Right
Rude	Assertive	Passive	Critical
Aggressive	Enthusiastic	Get Along	Stick to process
Win at all costs	Innovative	Good listener	Enforce rules
Wants to lead	Likes to lead	Team player	Withdrawn

Look at the list of works and count the number you selected in each **column**. Write the total for each column below:

Total words selected in each column:

The first column contains a list of words strongly associated with the D style for dominance, the second column contains a list of words strongly associated with the I style for influence, the third column contains a list of words strongly associated with the S style for steadiness, and the fourth column contains a list of words strongly associated with the C style for conscientiousness. Use the guide below to identify whether you are high, medium, or low across the four behavioural styles.

Style	Low	Medium	High
D	1-4	5-10	11-18
I	1-4	5-10	11-18
S	1-4	5-10	11-18
C	1-4	5-10	11-18

Now that you have a better understanding of your behavioural style and the potential impact it may have on your work environment and on the people you work with it is time to explore how to apply the DISC model in the workplace. In the next chapter we will explore how and when to use DISC to increase your effectiveness when dealing with interpersonal situations.

Chapter Seven: Applying DiSC

Introducing DiSC to the workplace.

7

Applying DiSC

Knowing about DiSC is one thing, but applying DiSC is another. To enhance your success in the workplace with interpersonal relationships use the DiSC model and adapt your style.

DISC is a powerful tool that can be used to increase your success and effectiveness in the workplace when dealing with interpersonal relationships. From communicating at meetings to managing performance, applying DISC and adapting your behavioural style will deliver increased success. Successful people understand the need to adapt and modify their behaviours to increase their success. You may recall in chapter 1 we discussed the importance of the three A's, which are to acknowledge, to accept, and to appreciate that people are different to you. Take a moment and just imagine if this were not true, if everyone in the world was exactly the same as you.

What do you think that would be like? Let's take a moment to explore that. If everyone in the world was exactly the same as you; you would no longer be able buy your favourite food as it will always be sold out, you would need to book your favourite holiday destination at least 10 years in advance as everyone else always wants to travel there too, and you can forget about your favourite hobby or pastime as these would be always overbooked and/or unavailable due to the amount of people who are taking part in these activities.

So as you can see the world would not be a great place if everyone was exactly the same as you, and this is without even exploring such things as creativity and diversity. Instead we live in a world where everyone is different we need to acknowledge this, we need to accept this, and we also need to appreciate this.

Because people are different that also means they have a different perception and understanding of the world around them. People's views and perceptions will be different from yours across a broad range of situations. For some people this can be a source of conflict and for others it can be a great source of creativity. The choice is yours, you can be frustrated and upset that people hold different views to yours or you can explore the differences in your perceptions to enhance your understanding of situations and help you achieve further success.

No one can be right about everything all of the time, you may feel quality is more important than quantity, whereas a work colleague may feel quantity outweighs the importance of quality. You need to acknowledge that you both have a difference of opinion on what is most important. When it comes to project work and teams you may place an emphasis on delivering the result, whereas other members of the project team may feel the relationships are more important than the result. Both of you have very valid points, the result is important, but so are the relationships. Without positive and supportive relationships, some people may argue, you will never achieve the result; on the other hand without the sense of achievement, some relationships may never develop high levels of trust and support.

We also need to accept these differences, there is no point in digging your heels in trying to prove that you are right all of the time. Remember when you believe you are right that means that everyone else who does not agree with you must be wrong, but remember those same people believe they are right and therefore since you do not agree with them you must be wrong. We can go round in circles for hours, days, months, years, debating who is right and who is wrong without ever agreeing or achieving a result.

You need to accept these differences and start to explore the other person's point of view before explaining your point of view. Take a look at the illustration below, these two people have been arguing for over 3000 years and they are no closer today to agreeing than they were when they began. Who do you think is right?

The person on the left is arguing that the object is concave while the person on the right believes it to be convex. As you can see they are both correct, from their point of view, the person on the left truly does see a concave shape, while the person on the right is correct that the shape they are looking at is convex. However, as you know they are both correct, but we have the advantages of seeing both perspectives. How could you resolve an argument such as this without being able to see both perspectives? What we typically see in the workplace is that all people are entrenched in their point of view and are not open to seeing the other's perspective.

To resolve an issue such as this, one of the two people need to take a look at the object from the perspective of the other person, only then will they see the full picture, but who is going to offer to take a look at the other person's perspective? This is the dilemma we face in the workplace when two people believe they are right and are unwilling to see the other person's perspective. When you find yourself in a situation such as this the powerful thing to do is to seek an understanding of the other person's perspective first. Remember the choice is yours you can try and force the other person to change their opinion or you can adapt and modify your behaviour and instead of arguing your point of view you can try to understand the other person's point of view. Once you have a fuller understanding from both sides then you reach a deeper understanding of the situation.

Finally we need to appreciate that people do have different perspectives and opinions. Sharing our differences and appreciating diversity can enable us to identify and explore new possibilities that we may have overlooked with just our own point of view. Remember just because somebody does not see something the same way as you do does not necessarily mean they are incorrect, they just see it differently to you. In certain situations this can be extremely powerful because you may be too close or too attached to a situation to be able to give an objective view.

The DISC model is built around the three A's helping you acknowledge, accept, and appreciate the diversity of different behaviours. When you are building relationships with people it is all too easy to insist that they change their behaviour or that they adapt to your needs and requirements, however successful people make the first move, they step around the corner to see the situation from the other person's perspective. DISC gives you the opportunity to do this.

In interpersonal situations where behaviours can be a cause of issues you have a range of choices that you can make. Just like our friends who have been arguing about the shape of the object for over 3000 years you can insist that the other person needs to change and expect them to change their behaviours, you can demand a change, and stick to your own behaviours. Or you can use your knowledge of DISC to change your own behaviours and adapt these behaviours to get the most success from the situation you are faced with.

By modifying and adapting your behaviours to suit the specific situation you are faced with you will achieve a much higher level of success in your interpersonal relationships. Whether you are trying to influence a staff member or gain commitment and buy in to a project idea adapting your behaviours to suit the situation will lead you to success.

For example, if your boss displays the behaviours of a high D style person and you need to discuss with them the allocation of resources and funding for an upcoming project, you may want to position your requests in such a way that the emphasis is on delivering the results. You may want to say something like *'to achieve the goal by the deadline here's what we need to do...'* Whereas if your boss displayed more of the behaviours related to a high I style person you may choose to craft your message so that it appeals to their behavioural style such as, *'hi Sam, thanks again for meeting me I wouldn't be able to do this without you. I've taken a look at the project and here's the help they need from you to make sure that we get this done so that everyone gives us a big thank you when it's finished'.*

On the other hand if your boss was more of a high S or a high C style you may also choose to craft your message so it would appeal to their behavioural style. Some people may argue that this style of approach is not authentic and that they should not change or adapt their behaviour to suit other people. Authenticity is highly important, it is about staying true to your values and achieving the results you desire. If you choose to modify and adapt your behaviours while still staying true to your values and achieving results why would you not want to do this. Remember modifying and adapting your behaviours is not about changing who you are, it's about changing how you do things to achieve more results.

Modifying and adapting your behaviours to suit the style of the other person and/or the situation that you face is a successful strategy for achieving results. The DISC model does not ask you to change who you are, more importantly it helps you understand how other people view the world and helps you appreciate what they value. Armed with this knowledge and understanding you can adapt and modify your behaviours to deal more effectively with this person to achieve your results.

Applying the disc model in the workplace is a simple three step process:

1. Assess the behavioural style of the other person to identify whether they are more of a D, I, S, or C.

2. Modifying/adapting behaviours in line with the behavioural needs of the style you have diagnosed. For example, if you believe the person is a high C make sure when you communicate with them that you are detailed, analytical, and articulate.

3. Gauge the response you get from the person, if it is a positive response you have successfully diagnosed the behaviour style, however, if the response is not aligned with what you expect from that specific behavioural style, try to reassess their behaviours and re-diagnose their style.

Remember to pay close attention to the needs and wants of each of the behavioural styles. In previous chapters we have discussed each of the styles and how they like to communicate, process information, deal with conflict, and how they may be influenced. Review this information and select the appropriate strategies for dealing with each of the behavioural styles face-to-face or through other communication channels.

Even when you are sending e-mails or written correspondence keep in mind the behavioural style of the recipient. The high D style wants the information summarised and to the point. The high I style wants a focus on the enthusiasm, motivation, and engagement. The S style wants to avoid conflict or disharmony, they like information to be steady and nonthreatening. The high C style likes to see all the facts and figures and wants to see the detail.

In the next chapter we will start to explore the use of DISC when dealing with difficult people. As discussed in the previous chapter when people are outside their comfort zone or not achieving their desired results they have the potential to display difficult behaviours. The DISC model can also help us understand and overcome these difficult behaviours so as to help us achieve results.

Chapter Eight: Dealing With Difficult People

Understanding the motivation behind the behaviours

8

Dealing with Difficult People

We can all be difficult from time to time, when we are under pressure or when we are tired and frustrated. Difficult behaviours can be dealt with through knowledge and understanding of the DiSC model.

Difficult people are the ones we cannot stand to be around, their behaviours drive us mad. They never seem to do what you want them to do and they are always causing you stress and difficulty. We cannot understand or accept their behaviour as we think it is not appropriate. We can be frightened of their behaviours if they are forceful and bullying, frustrated if they are stubborn or demanding, annoyed if they are self-centred, or agitated if they are a know it all.

Difficult people come with a range of difficult behaviours. This chapter will look at the 12 most common difficult behaviours found in the workplace. We will explore and define these 'Dirty Dozen' of difficult behaviours, understand where they come from, and identify the intent behind the behaviours.

The Dirty Dozen
(the 12 most difficult behaviours)

The Bully

Pushy and ruthless, loud and forceful, the bully knows what he/she wants and how to get it. If you are in their way or standing against them they will either cut you down or steamroll over you. They are single minded and not afraid to focus in like a laser on a person or issue. There is no discussion with the bully, it is their way or no way.

The Sniper

Operates behind your back taking pot-shots at you or your credibility. They seek out your weaknesses and exploit them. In the workplace they covertly work against you. For some reason they resent you or your position. They don't get mad, they get even.

The Volcano

Like a ticking time-bomb you are just waiting for this person to explode. When they do it is always disproportionate to the situation. Everyone around them tries to head for higher ground and escape the torrent of their venting.

The Expert

The expert knows everything, just ask them, actually you won't have to! They are always telling you and not listening to a word you say since your ideas are not as good as theirs.

The Bluffer

The bluffer tries to show he/she is an expert at everything. No matter what the topic or situation is they will have an input and boast of their experience in this area. They often give the wrong information or advice but never admit responsibility.

The Agreer (Agree-er)

Always saying yes, but often leaving you disappointed the agreer over commits and under delivers. They are always trying to please everyone by agreeing with them, even when agreeing is in contradiction to a previous agreement!

The Avoider

Go on; just try to get the avoider to make a decision. They are the experts in procrastination; every question is answered with a 'maybe'. They never commit and avoid taking action. The avoider believes that if they wait long enough someone else will make the decision or take action.

The Void

You just cannot tell what is going on because the void tells you nothing, no feedback, no verbal hints, no body language, just a blank response. The more you push the less you get. Getting anything out of the void is like drawing blood from a stone.

The Doomsayer

'This won't work, that won't work' and 'no, that's no good' are just some of the doomsayer's favourite sayings. They have the ability to see what is wrong with everything. They are very negative to any new ideas but defend their actions by saying they are just being realistic. The doomsayer is discouraging and sees a cloud on every silver lining.

The Whinger

The world is against this person and they love telling everyone about it. The whinger constantly whines about everything and everyone, they love to wallow in their own woe. No matter what you say to the whinger they will complain about it. The whinger believes it is all everyone else's fault and they are not prepared to do anything about it except whinge.

The Controller

This person wants to do everything and be involved in everything. They love to take control. If you are managing a project and they are on the team, watch them take over and try to control everything. They do this in front of you and behind your back. You arrive into work finding they have changed your plan or schedule without asking.

The Waster

You know this person does nothing but no one seems to do anything about it. While everyone else is busy they swan around talking about how busy they are but never doing anything. When you ask them to help out they have a hundred and one excuses why they cannot help. When their work is late/not done again they have a list of excuses, it is never their fault.

Did you recognise anyone in the list? Maybe you recognised a few people, or the same person with a few of the behaviours. If your work colleagues read the list would they recognise you?

These are the 12 most difficult behaviours in the workplace that people have to deal with on a regular basis. Difficult people are not limited to this 'Dirty Dozen' of behaviours, however, these are the top 12 most common difficult behaviours taken from research in the workplace.

As stated in the previous chapter we can all be difficult from time to time when our needs are not being met or when we are frustrated, however, difficult behaviours are more regular and systemic. Difficult people display these behaviours on a regular basis. To deal effectively with these behaviours and get difficult people to be less difficult it is important to understand the intent behind each of the behaviours. As you will see the intent is positive it is just the impact of the behaviours that is difficult. When we understand the intent behind someone's behaviours we can better deal with their behaviours. Instead of just judging them on their behaviour, we have a deeper understanding and can see why they are behaving this way. We may not agree with it, but we can understand it. This helps use to be able to deal more effectively with the difficult behaviour.

The next chapter will explore specific strategies for dealing with each of the 12 difficult behaviours, for now we need to explore and understand the intent behind the 12 behaviours. To help you reach a better understanding of the intent behind the behaviours we will relate them to the DISC model and identify the underlying needs and motivation behind each of the DISC behavioural styles.

Exploring the intent /motivation behind the DISC behaviours:

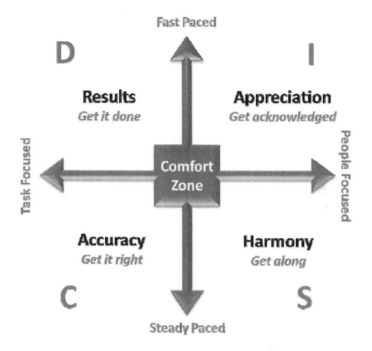

Understanding the four intents:

* **D** – *Dominance – Results, get it done*
* **I** – *Influence – Appreciation, get acknowledged*
* **S** – *Steadiness – Harmony, get along*
* **C** – *Conscientiousness- Accuracy, get it right*

Results:
The D-style behaviours are a result of the underlying need and motivation to get it done and achieve a result. The positive side of this motivation is the focus on results, the innovation and drive for achievement and the ability to overcome difficult

situations and/or issues. The negative side of this motivation is the pushy and dominant behaviours that are displayed when the D-style is not achieving their goal of results, getting it done.

Appreciation:
The I-style behaviours are a result of the underlying need and motivation to get acknowledged and receive appreciation. The positive side of this motivation is the focus on enthusiasm, collaboration, innovation, engagement and action. The negative side of this motivation is the attention seeking, the sulking, the sniping, and the self-centred behaviours that are displayed when the I-style is not achieving their goal of appreciation, getting acknowledged.

Harmony:
The S-style behaviours are a result of the underlying need and motivation to get along and achieve harmony. The positive side of this motivation is the focus on team work, listening, collaboration, and support. The negative side of this motivation is the withdrawn, passive, approval seeking and submissive behaviours that are displayed when the S-style is not achieving their goal of harmony, getting along.

Accuracy:
The C-style behaviours are a result of the underlying need and motivation to get it right and achieve accuracy. It is also important to understand that 'getting it right' also includes justice, or at least the C's perception of justice. The positive side of this motivation is the focus on accuracy, stability,

challenge, quality, and analysis. The negative side of this motivation is the picky, perfectionist, negative, and stubborn behaviours that are displayed when the C-style is not achieving their goal of accuracy, getting it right.

Intents continuously change, depending on the person and the situation, which brings changes in behaviour. It helps to:

1. **Understand the four intents:**
   They all have their time and place in our lives.

2. **Be attentive to communications:**
   Be aware of words, tone, and body language, they can indicate primary intent.

3. **Don't be difficult:**
   When your intents are not met, you may become a difficult person yourself.

When each of the DISC styles are achieving their underlying needs they are in the comfort zone and have the flexibility to interact effectively with all other styles. Once our basic needs are being met we are more tolerable of the people and situations around us.

It is only when the underlying needs are not being met that we start to see the difficult behaviours emerging. Remember that when we are under stress or not achieving our needs we revert to type, or return to norm, meaning we become MORE of our primary DISC style. The D becomes more of a D, the I more of an I, the S more of an S, and the C more of a C. When the underlying needs are not being met people move away from the comfort zone and become less flexible in their approach and behaviours.

Relating the behaviours to the Intents:

Below you will find a basic model relating each of the 12 difficult behaviours to the corresponding intent. It is important to understand that we can display any of the behaviours in a specific situation; the list below shows the most common relationship between the intent and the behaviours.

The Intent	The associated behaviours
Results – Get it Done	The Bully
	The Expert
	The Sniper
	The Controller

The Intent	The associated behaviours
Appreciation – Get acknowledged	The Sniper
	The Volcano
	The Bluffer
	The Waster

The Intent	The associated behaviours
Harmony – Get along	The Volcano
	The Agreer
	The Avoider
	The Void

The Intent	The associated behaviours
Accuracy – Get it right	The Expert
	The Void
	The Doomsayer
	The Whinger

Understanding the behaviours under pressure:

If people are out of their comfort zone for too long they will exaggerate their behavioural style. This is a warning sign, when you observe these behaviours it is time to address them directly and try to help the person achieve their underlying needs. Here are the exaggerated behaviours:

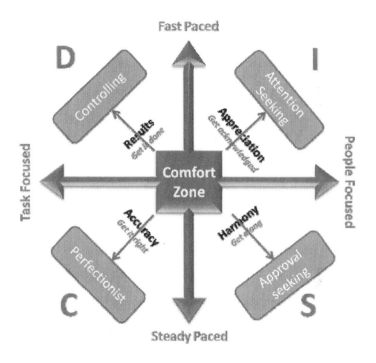

- *D* – *Dominance* – *becomes controlling*
- *I* – *Influence* – *becomes attention seeking*
- *S* – *Steadiness* – *becomes approval seeking*
- *C* – *Conscientiousness- becomes a perfectionist*

Controlling:

The D-style becomes more controlling, they micro-manage everyone and everything. They want all of the details and they want them now. If you cannot give them what they want they will get it themselves. Usually happy with just the bullet points the D-style looks for more and more detail as they become more controlling.

Attention seeking:

Starved of appreciation the I-style will jump and shout until they get attention. This is a cry for help, they are simply stating *'look at me, acknowledge me...'* this may be in the form of over exaggerated behaviours or out of context responses and actions. They may jump in with a smart or snide comment just to get noticed. They can also explode and rant about a situation.

Approval seeking:

Remember the last thing the S-style wants to do is cause conflict, so when they are out of their comfort zone too long they start to seek approval for everything. They do not want to do anything without external approval first just in case it may add to the disharmony.

Perfection seeking:

The C-style will become overly negative and criticise everyone and everything as it falls way below their inflexible standards. They will not be happy until everything is 100%, 99.9% will not do. They become overbearing with the finite details and set unrealistic standards of expectation. Meanwhile they constantly complain that no one cares.

It is important to remember that we can all be difficult from time to time, but when these difficult behaviours become the norm then we become difficult people.

Keep an eye out for the behaviours of the 'Dirty Dozen':

In the next chapter we will explore a range of strategies designed to bring out the best in these difficult behaviours.

Chapter Nine: Bringing out the best in people

Strategies for dealing with difficult people

9

Bringing out the best in people

When it comes to getting the best out of difficult people it is about addressing the behaviour, not the person. We can all have difficult behaviours from time to time, however, when they become the normal behaviour it is time to change your approach and use a new model for success.

Difficult behaviours can cause stress, frustration, and dismay for the people who have to deal with them. If you are on the receiving end of a difficult behaviour you know how it can make you feel. This chapter will introduce you to a range of proven strategies that are designed to bring the best out of people when they are stuck in their difficult behaviour. From changing your mindset and approach to communicating and tactics these strategies will help you deal with difficult people.

Choosing your approach:

1. Understand that everybody reacts differently to these types of behaviour.

The person who's most irritating to you may be perfectly acceptable to someone else.

2. Get to know these people.

Each warrants a different response. Think about the people you know. Does anybody at work or at home display these behaviours?

3. Recognise when you are difficult.

We can all be difficult at times. Understanding these behaviours in yourself will help you understand them in others.

You do have a choice about how you deal with difficult people, actually you have a range of choices, they are:

- *Just put up with it -stay and do nothing*
- *Walk away -vote with your feet*
- *View them differently -change your attitude*
- *Treat them differently -change your behaviour*

Avoid doing nothing. Only walk away when it is the best option. Work on changing your attitude and then your behaviour. You will be amazed at the results.

Even if the difficult person continues to engage in the difficult behaviour, you can learn to see them differently, listen to them differently, and feel differently about them.

A 5-Step approach:

When you need to deal with difficult people and their behaviours here is a simple 5-step approach to increasing your effectiveness:

1. Reduce barriers and differences
2. Listen closely to understand
3. Explore and understand
4. Communicate clearly
5. Focus on the positive and improvement

Reduce barriers and differences

Remember that no one cooperates with anyone who seems to be against him or her.

- Blend your voice and body language to match the other person.
- Blend before you redirect. Only after building rapport can you redirect.
- Match the level of their energy and reflect the emotions they are expressing.
- Use the same language and sayings.
- Talk about 'US' not you and them, remove barriers and differences.

Conflict occurs when the emphasis is on differences. Reducing differences can turn conflict into cooperation.

Listen closely to understand

It is twice as hard to listen than it is to speak, listen hard and listen well. Only when someone feels they are being listening to will they open up and communicate.

- Learn and practice active listening.
- Listen- Show you are listening – ask clarifying questions, summarise, and confirm.
- Make sure the other person knows you have heard and understood.

When two or more people want to be heard and no one is willing to listen, an argument is inevitable. Listen and understand first, and you unlock the doors to understanding and collaboration.

Explore and understand

Seek clarity and understanding of the intent behind the words or behaviours. Try to explore the 'why'. Put yourself in their shoes and see it from their point of view.

- Identify and act on the intent.
- Use criteria to reach deeper understanding. What are the filters (yours and theirs), how can you by-pass these.

This is about the kind of understanding that will help you communicate effectively. Understanding from their point of view will help you create solutions that match.

Communicate clearly

Use simple words and phrases, state the facts, give examples, and check for clarity.

- Monitor your tone of voice, tactfully interrupt, and tell your truth.
- Remember that the word 'communicate' has the same origins as' common' –to communicate is to build a common understanding.

What you say to people can produce defensiveness or trust, increase resistance or cooperation, promote conflict or understanding. Make sure you are focusing on the responses you want to invoke.

Focus on the positive and improvement

Understand and embrace ***Pygmalion power***, when you tell someone that they are doing something wrong, they are very likely to get defensive, when you focus on the positive and the required improvement it promotes a positive response.

- Appreciate criticism; this is nothing more than the flip of Pygmalion power.
- It's a fact that people rise or fall to the level of your expectations and projections.

Project and expect the best, remember we see the behaviours we are looking for. Start to look for the positive behaviours, you may just surprise yourself.

Bringing the best out of: **The Bully**

Bringing the best out of: **The Bully**

The Intent

Remember the intent behind the behaviour of the bully is to get it done, they are focusing on results. They need it done now and if you are in the way they will push you aside or push straight through you to get the result.

From their point of view:

The bully is on a mission to get it done, they are unable to slow down or change behaviours as they do not see anything wrong with what they are doing. If you are in the way you need to be removed. They have no problem with pulling you apart personally, however, it is not personal, you just happen to be in the way of them achieving their result.

How to deal with 'The Bully':

If you are under attack from the bully they probably see you as part of the problem. Their aggressive behaviour is to get you doing what they want or get you out of the way and let them do it themselves. Here is what you need to do:

1. Don't back down
2. Take control, interrupt them
3. Address the main issue
4. Focus on results
5. Agree actions

Don't back down:

If you fold like a deckchair the bully will see this as a win and learn that to deal with you all they have to do is push harder.

We give people permission to treat us the way they do through our behaviours and responses. If the bully learns that you agree or get out of the way when they push harder or shout louder then they are going to do this when you are in the way! Stand your ground, you do not need to counter-attack, just stay with your position. Let the bully rant and rave and when they are finished look them in the eye, state your position and move to the next step.

Take control, interrupt them:

If the bully is not giving up and they start all over again when you state your position then you need to take control and interrupt them. A very effective way of doing this is by repeating their names over and over until you have their attention. Stay very assertive (aggressive people actually respect assertive people), keep your voice to about ¾ of the level they are speaking at. Now that you have their attention it is time to move to the next step.

Address the main issue:

Backtrack to the main issue the bully has and address it directly, this shows you were listening and are interested in their concerns. Explain how you understand the situation and ask them to clarify the situation. If they start to rant and rave again go back to the previous step. When they start to explain their perception of the issue make sure you do not judge their opinion, you only want to show you are addressing the same issue as the bully. Now it is time to switch the focus to results.

Focus on results:

Turn the conversation towards what you can and will do. If this is not enough for the bully clearly state again what you can and will do. Even in situations where you totally disagree with the bully tell them exactly what you are going to do. This may simply be ' *I am not going to do that'*, *'here is what I am going to do'*. Keep your language focused towards results, for example, if they are asking you to do something that requires additional resources instead of saying *'I can't do that because...'* say *'to do that I will need...'*.

Agree actions

Finally agree actions, who will do what and by when. Make sure it is clear who is responsible for the actions. In situations where you have stated you are not going to do what they want, use this step to agree what they need to do next, and how they need to behave with you going forward, for example, ' *we can't agree on this, you need to find another way to achieve this and when you are ready to discuss this normally I will be here to help you achieve the result'*.

Actions to avoid:

- Never counter-attack the bully.
- Don't defend, explain, or justify your position, just state it assertively.
- Don't shut down, you may be tempted to withdraw but this will send a clear message of victory to the bully and reinforce their difficult behaviour.

Bringing the best out of: **The Sniper**

Bringing the best out of: **The Sniper**

The Intent

Remember the intent behind the behaviour of the sniper is to get results or to get acknowledged. When the intent is to get results they are using the behaviour of a sniper to control your actions, when the intent is to get acknowledged they are using the behaviour to pull you down and replace you as the centre of attention.

From their point of view:

The sniper has a grudge against you, either they cannot approach you directly or they feel they have to discredit you first. You have what they want and you do not deserve it. Either you hold the key to their goal or you are stealing their limelight. Either way they will try to take you down through covert operations working behind your back to help others see you the same way they do.

How to deal with 'The Sniper':

If you wronged a sniper in some way here is what you need to do:

1. Draw attention to them
2. Ask questions
3. Be assertive, (*use bully strategy if required*)
4. Find out why
5. Agree the future

Draw attention to them:

Your goal is to bring the sniper out of hiding and shine a light on them. Draw attention to their behaviour, even if this is in the middle of a meeting, stop what you are doing, look at them and repeat the comment they said. Remember the sniper likes to take 'pot-shots' at you, especially when you appear vulnerable. If you overhear the sniper saying *'that is a stupid idea'*, stop, look at them and ask *'why do you think this is a stupid idea'*. Once you engage with them it is time to ask questions. If the sniper is deep under cover and you are only hearing the snipes from distance (never catching them in the act), then make it known you are aware of their behaviours. At meetings state you are aware that someone (keep it focused on the individual not a group, never say I am aware that some people are saying...) is saying this or that...

Ask questions:

When you confront the sniper start to ask very assertive and direct questions such as, *'why do you think that?'* or *'what is really behind you comments here?'*. Keep your tone neutral and adopt an inquisitive stance, show that you really do want to know why they feel/think this way.

Be assertive:

Face the sniper head on, if they revert to typical bully behaviours (becoming aggressive, raising their voice, dismissing your questions etc.) then switch to the strategy for dealing with the bully. If they start to complain or get defensive don't let them off with a warning, stay assertive until you identify what the real issue is. You do not need to attack them, just stay assertive, the added attention will draw out their true intention and help you understand if you are dealing with someone who resents you or someone who feels you are in their way for some reason.

Find out why:

Keep using questions to uncover the real issue behind their behaviour. If you do not uncover the issue or address it they will just go on sniping at you afterwards. If they will not answer you directly or are deep under cover then ask open questions to the other people. The goal is to find out why and to understand it. Do not judge their opinion or defend your position, simply try to understand why they feel this way.

Agree the future:

Finally, agree with the sniper what you can and will do. Address their concerns and explain what you expect from them in the future. Make it clear you will not tolerate sniper behaviour and encourage them to come to you directly next time.

Be aware of the 'friendly sniper':

There is another type of sniper; the 'friendly' sniper. Very common in cultures such as Ireland where 'slagging' and sarcasm are part of normal humour. If you become the target of a friendly sniper then simply ignore the comment, laugh with it, or if you feel it is not appropriate then snipe back with good humour, turn the comment back on them in a fun way. For example if they say ' *that's another one of them stupid ideas that management are always coming up with...*' then respond quickly with a witty comment such as ' *well we have to work hard in management to keep up with the crazy ideas you come out with.. How are we doing by the way?*'

Bringing the best out of: **The Volcano**

Bringing the best out of: **The Volcano**

The Intent

The volcano's behaviour can be driven by their need to get attention and be acknowledged or their need for harmony. Either way they have had enough and their emotions have taken over.

From their point of view:

Enough is enough, they have tried everything they could think of to change the situation but nothing has worked. No one seems to care about the situation or them. How can people allow this to go on this way, it is just not fair. They have had enough; there is no way they can put up with the current situation any longer. This is truly the '*straw that broke the camel's back*'...

How to deal with 'The Volcano':

When they explode they explode on a major scale, this is no simple gripe or whim, they have lost control of rational thinking and they are driven by their emotions, here is what you need to do:

1. Get their attention
2. Show you care
3. Bring them down
4. Let them cool off
5. Don't stoke the fire

Get their attention:

Stand in front of them, call their name, put a gentle hand on their upper arm (be aware of people's personal space needs).

Do whatever you need to get their attention without coming across as aggressive. Make sure your tone of voice is not angry or demanding, you need to come across as concerned and in control. Repeat their name over and over if you need to. If they have stormed off while erupting then you need to make a decision to either go after them if you feel it is right to, or to leave them to cool off and discuss it with them at a later point.

Show you care:

Remember they are highly emotional right now and not typically open to logic or reasoning. The first thing you need to do once you have their attention is show them you care about how they are feeling. Match their intensity but not the emotion. Tell them you can see they are very upset and you want to help, ask them to explain what has happened and help you understand how they are feeling. Listen closely and provide reassurance as they speak. Never judge their reasons just listen and understand.

Bring them down:

As you notice them calming down, start to lower your voice and try to reduce the intensity, allow them to talk it out. Just by listening you are helping them to become calm. Never judge them or start to tell them what they should be doing, just listen and reassure them. The time for addressing the issue and/or behaviour comes later; your focus now is to get them back in control of their emotions. Keep your tone encouraging and make sure you are using non aggressive body language (avoid pointing or making negative facial gestures).

Let them cool off:

If their adrenaline is still pumping and you feel the time is not right to discuss alternative behaviour or to address the issue without them exploding all over again then give them some time to cool off. Let them know you are doing this by saying *'I can see how passionate you are about this right now, why don't you take some time to gather your thoughts and we can discuss this later, say about 3pm, we can grab a coffee or I can drop down to your desk...'* if they are already cool enough and you feel addressing the issue will not set them off again then calmly discuss the issue and or situation with them.

Don't stoke the fire:

Try to identify what sets this person off, why do they explode and where possible avoid setting them off or 'stoking the fire' by bringing up situations and/or issues you know will cause them to erupt. You do not need to 'walk on egg shells' if the situation or issue that sets them off is a normal work situation that is part of the day to day life of their role then additional training/coaching or communication around this is required.

Actions to avoid:

- Don't get aggressive with the volcano, even when you think their behaviour is selfish.
- Avoid judging them on this interaction alone, remember this may be a build up of many things, and make sure you get to know them and what they value.
- Don't isolate them or treat them differently to others, help them integrate and adapt.

Bringing the best out of: **The Expert**

Bringing the best out of: **The Expert**

The Intent

The behaviour of the expert is driven by the need to get the right result; they are the expert and know exactly what needs to be done. They will either dismiss your inferior ideas or tell you at length why they are inferior. This particular behaviour commonly shares the intent of get it done (results) and get it right (accuracy).

From their point of view:

The expert knows they are the expert, they are number one and everyone else is a distant second. They get frustrated by other people not doing the job to the expert standards they are used to. Why can't everyone else just do it the way they do, it is the best way after all. They have to waste time showing or telling everyone exactly how it is done.

How to deal with 'The Expert':

The expert has a proven track record of being right 99.9% of the time, like it or not, you have to respect their expertise and knowledge in their field. The easiest way to bring the best out the expert is by the following strategy:

1. Do your research
2. Acknowledge their expertise
3. Share their concerns
4. Suggest ideas indirectly
5. Use their strengths

Do your research:

Make sure you have your facts and information correct before you approach the expert, do your homework/research first.

If you are unsure of a topic or what you need to address the expert will rip through the flaws in your idea. Make sure you have a logical approach that deals with facts and figures, avoid bringing in emotions or personal opinions. The expert enjoys a good debate when the focus is on facts and logic. The expert will try to make you feel inferior so earn their respect by showing you have prepared well for this interaction and that you are knowledgeable in this area.

Acknowledge their expertise:

Let them know you respect their knowledge and expertise. Reassure them that they are the expert in this area and that you want to discuss an idea with them to improve efficiency or effectiveness. You are looking for their input to the idea to perfect it. Allow them to give you their ideas, where they are dismissive of your idea, ask them what they would do to achieve the desired outcome. If you want them to listen to your idea and not dismiss it straight off you need to make sure the expert sees how their input is required in this area.

Share their concerns:

If the expert is complaining about the current situation and/or idea, share their concerns, explore why they are concerned about the situation and/or idea. Try to identify if their primary intent is to get it done or to get it right. Once you have identified their primary intent and their main concerns you can blend your language and approach to address these areas directly. Explain how your idea will achieve the result or accuracy they desire, and also reduce or remove their concerns.

Suggest ideas indirectly:

Now it is time to redirect the expert to your idea, however, you need to do this indirectly. Saying straight out *'here is what I think you should do...'* will only send the expert back to step 1 where they see your idea as inferior. Use language such as *'maybe', 'perhaps', 'what would happen if'* and *'we'* instead of *'I'*. Avoid challenging them directly, try to introduce your ideas as alternatives to achieving the same goals.

Use their strengths:

One of the things the expert enjoys is showing/telling others how to do it right. Encourage them to do this now with the new idea. Turn them into a mentor by asking them to make sure everyone is up to speed and proficient on this new task or process. Get them focused on showing/telling others about the idea. Also from time to time go to them for advice, let them know you respect their knowledge. Over time they will begin to see you as a peer and not someone who is inferior to them.

Actions to avoid:

* Resist being a 'know it all' yourself when engaging with an expert this will just focus them on proving you wrong.
* Don't resent the expert; they are a valuable asset to everyone when focused in the right direction.
* Never try to force your ideas on to the expert, take your time, be flexible and patient.

Bringing the best out of: **The Bluffer**

Bringing the best out of: **The Bluffer**

The Intent

The bluffer is looking for attention and appreciation. They are driven by the need to be acknowledged. There is nothing more the bluffer loves than to be told *'we couldn't have done this without you!'*.

From their point of view:

The bluffer really wants to help out, they love being the centre of attention and having everything revolve around them. They want to help out everywhere even if the area is not their field of expertise. From time to time they get in over their heads in a situation but they do not want to lose face or have you think they cannot help so they try to bluff their way out of it. It's easier to come up with an excuse than admit they are wrong or do not know.

How to deal with 'The Bluffer':

The bluffer can cause untold damage to tasks and teams by leading people in the wrong direction, they can also build a reputation where people automatically dismiss their input due to past experiences, to get the best out of the bluffer try this:

1. Acknowledge them
2. Get specific
3. Take control
4. Let them off
5. Acknowledge what they can do

Acknowledge them:

Acknowledge their intent and enthusiasm; let them know you appreciate their help and involvement. This will relax them.

You want to create a friendly environment for the bluffer, remember one of their biggest fears is losing face or thinking people are against them. Try to acknowledge any recent successes they have had or contributed towards. Once they are comfortable turn your attention to the issue at hand.

Get specific:

Ask them to explain the current situation, what happened and what they think about it. Try to get them to be specific, the bluffer will tend to generalise and blame other people, however, you need to redirect them back to the specifics and their input and/or responsibilities. If the information they are giving you is misleading or wrong direct them back to what is correct and explore the areas they are wrong about. Give them suggestions and hints towards the correct answers and try to allow them to discover the right answers themselves. If they are unable to do this and maintain their position then it is time to take control and explain the right course of action.

Take control:

If the bluffer is not taking the hint and they continue to bluff then it is time to step in and take control. Interrupt the bluffer politely and tell them the right course of action or the correct answer. You do not need to 'rub it in their face', simply state *'here is what I think you should do...'* explain why you think this is the right course of action and get them to acknowledge it. If needed you can position it *as 'if you did this... that would be great and the team would be really thankful to you'.* Make sure they know and understand what you have asked them to do, and get them to tell you how they will do it.

Let them off:

Above all, don't make the bluffer feel you are calling their bluff in an aggressive way. There is no need to back them into a corner and have them admit they are wrong, this is not going to help the situation, it may make you feel good, but remember you want to get the best out the bluffer so focus them on the correct course of action and let them off. It may help to focus on their positive intent, after all they are only trying to help.

Acknowledge what they can do:

Bluffers quickly build up a reputation of being a 'think they know it all' and people start to avoid them and/or dismiss their input without considering it. This is a dangerous cycle for two reasons, 1- you may dismiss a good idea, and 2- the lack of appreciation will only cause them to seek out more attention and increase these difficult behaviours. Try to acknowledge what they are good at, focus on their achievements and encourage their enthusiasm.

Actions to avoid:

- Try to avoid 'bursting their bubble' if you challenge them directly they will only bluff more or make excuses.
- Never judge them too quickly, a bluffer is not always a bluffer, they can be experts in some areas, listen to their input first and reflect before making a snap judgement.

Bringing the best out of: **The Agreer**

Bringing the best out of: **The Agreer**

The Intent

The last thing the agreer wants to do is upset anyone so they tend to say yes to every request. This behaviour is driven by the intent to get along and create harmony. They want to please you and this causes them to make promises they can not keep.

From their point of view:

The agreer really wants to help everyone, they are already snowed under themselves, but since they do not want to push back or upset anyone else they continually say yes to every request. As they are trying to do everything for everyone they typically end up finishing nothing for anybody.

How to deal with 'The Agreer':

The agreer can cause a critical project or task to be delayed, they are unable to meet deadlines due to the amount of work they are trying to undertake, however, when you approach them about it they reassure you it will be done, but it rarely is. Here is what you need to do:

1. Create a safe zone
2. Look for honesty
3. Help them focus
4. Agree small steps
5. Build the relationship

Create a safe zone:

Since the agreer wants harmony above all else you need to create a safe environment for them to discuss issues and challenges. They want to avoid causing problems or issues.

Because of this they will be uncomfortable opening up and discussing what they can and cannot do. Make sure your tone is suitable and your non-verbal communication is welcoming. Let them know it is safe to say 'no' and to push back on requests. Ask them to review what they are currently working on and realistically what they can deliver, and more importantly what they cannot deliver.

Look for honesty:

The agreer will have 101 reasons why they cannot deliver. Avoid the temptation to start giving them solutions to each problem, instead talk honestly and openly to the agreer about their ability to deliver on their commitments. Ask them to explore why they are saying yes to everything and help them to identify a process for planning. If the agreer becomes upset or angry, let them talk it out and move back to step 1 and focus on creating a safe communication environment.

Help them focus:

The agreer needs to develop skills in planning and prioritisation. Help them through this process, give them examples of planning tools and walk them through the steps required. Discuss different prioritisation tools and see which one suits the agreer best. Ask them to work through a few examples based on their current workload and commitments. Encourage them to use a daily to-do list with prioritisation, this will also allow them to push back on requests and focus on following through with their existing commitments. Have them practice saying no by applying the prioritisation tool to a set of typical requests.

Agree small steps:

The next step is to gain commitment from the agreer on how they are going to change their behaviours. Remember it will be difficult for them to change completely over night so agree small steps where they can build up the competence over a period of time. Start with the simple steps to give them confidence and reassurance. Agree to meet on a weekly basis to review how they are doing.

Build the relationship:

The agreer responds best to people and relationships, use every opportunity to build the relationship you currently have with them. Acknowledge their commitment and celebrate their achievements (no matter how small), make sure they understand how this new approach is helping everyone overall.

Actions to avoid:

* Avoid directly blaming the agreer as this will only make them feel ashamed and cause them to revert back to the difficult behaviour to try and please you.
* Never be impatient, remember it takes time to change behaviour.
* Don't remove the help and support too early; the agreer may revert back to previous behaviours. Make sure you stick with it. Give them enough support and help until you notice they are comfortable then start to reduce the support slowly over time.

Bringing the best out of: **The Avoider**

Bringing the best out of: **The Avoider**

The Intent

One of the last things the avoider wants to do is upset anyone so they tend to avoid committing to situations where they feel it will cause conflict or problems. This behaviour is driven by the intent to get along and create harmony. They avoid decisions hoping if they wait long enough the decision will make itself or someone else will make it for them.

From their point of view:

The avoider feels stuck in the middle, they can see both sides of an argument and want to agree with both sides to avoid any conflict. They don't want to have to pick and choose between the two sides as this will lead to conflict with the losing side.

How to deal with 'The Avoider':

The avoider sits between procrastination and indecision. They seem to be unable to make a decision especially if it is a critical one. Their typical language is '*maybe*' and '*I'll get back to you*'. When dealing with the avoider here is what you should do:

1. Create a safe zone
2. Find out why
3. Help them make decisions
4. Offer support
5. Build the relationship

Create a safe zone:

Since the avoider wants harmony above all else you need to create a safe environment for them to discuss issues and challenges. They want to avoid causing problems or issues.

Because of this they will be uncomfortable opening up and discussing why they are unable to make a decision. Make sure your tone is suitable and your non-verbal communication is welcoming and non-judgemental. Let them know it is safe to discuss issues and problems, this is not about taking sides, it is about understanding issues and finding solutions. Help them understand that by making a decision they are helping others, and by avoiding the decision they are only frustrating both sides.

Find out why:

It is important to surface any conflicts they currently have or are aware of. Help them understand how focusing on the decision will reduce the conflict, it is about the task not the person. Listen carefully to their concerns, where you hear words like *'I think so'*, *'maybe'* or 'that *could be'* this is a signal to dig deeper and seek clarification, try to understand their view of the situation and what they feel may happen. Once you have explored the reasons as to why they are avoiding the decision it is time to help them make the decision.

Help them make decisions:

Show them a range of decision making processes; find a number of processes that fit their needs. Walk them through the steps of decision making focusing on separating the people from the process (it is not about people, it is about the decision). Have them try out a few processes on a current decision they are avoiding and explore the potential outcomes. Get them to commit to a few decisions now.

Offer support:

Once the decision is made show them how you are going to support the decision, help them understand that there is no perfect decision in all situations. They need to make a decision based on the current information. Offer support in discussing future decisions over the short term (but avoid setting up a routine where they come to you for EVERY decision). Where they are still struggling with decisions it may be helpful to suggest training and/or coaching to develop these skills.

Build the relationship:

The avoider responds best to people and relationships, use every opportunity to build the relationship you currently have with them. Acknowledge their commitment to making a decision and celebrate their achievements (no matter how small), make sure they understand how this new approach is helping everyone overall. Seek them out from time to time to help with your decisions, show them you respect their new ability to make decisions.

Actions to avoid:

- Never push them for a quick decision, allow them to take 'reasonable' time to explore the options first.
- Do not lose your temper, you need to stay calm and focused, help the avoider understand it is not about the people and emotions, it is about the decision and actions.
- Try to resist applying too much pressure for a decision. Use the steps covered to help them reach crucial decisions.

Bringing the best out of: **The Void**

Bringing the best out of: **The Void**

The Intent

The void will typically withdraw in difficult situations, however, this behaviour may be driven by the need for harmony or accuracy. When the intent is to get along and create harmony the behaviour is to avoid conflict. When the intent is about justice and getting it right the behaviour is to avoid the wrong outcome, or at least attachment to the wrong outcome.

From their point of view:

The void chooses to withdraw and give little or no input as they are uncomfortable with the current situation, either they feel it is wrong or they are concerned about the impact of the outcome on people. They strongly believe the saying '*if you have nothing nice to say then say nothing at all*'.

How to deal with 'The Void':

It can be like drawing blood from a stone, but you need to get input from the void, there is no quick fix but here is a strategy that will help you achieve your goal:

1. Take your time
2. Explore for information
3. Probe for reasons
4. Guess their thoughts
5. State the impact

Take your time:

Dealing successfully with the void may take a long time. If you are in a rush or working under a time constraint, you may be too intense to draw him/her out. The more intense you are the more the void will withdraw and offer nothing in response. Plan ahead and pick a time and location that will give you at least an hour of undisrupted time to work through the situation with the void. It may also help to send an email and/or memo in advance fully describing what you would like to talk about and why. The wording of this email/memo is critical, it needs to be open and inviting, the focus should be on discussion and understanding, exploring the situation, you do not want to push for an outcome as this will only cause the void to withdraw further and build up a strong barrier before the meeting.

Explore for information:

Ask open ended questions when engaging with the void. They will try to use as few words as possible so do not make their task easier by asking closed questions. Your focus is on drawing them out and exploring the intent behind their behaviour. You want to find out if their behaviour is about justice (the right/wrong thing to do) or harmony (avoiding conflict with or towards people).

Probe for reasons:

If you are not getting a response from the void then switch to probing for reasons, ask more focused and leading questions to spark a response. Do not over do it with closed, assumptive questions at this stage, you just want to try and probe until you hit a soft spot, look for reaction (as there is usually none) to your statements or questions, this may indicate their intent.

Guess their thoughts:

If all else fails try to guess what their thoughts are, use assumptive statements, put yourself in their shoes and think out the situation and say what you think they may be thinking about it. Talk out loud and rattle of ideas and suggestions. Explore both intents, justice, and harmony, to see if you can get anything from them. Make bold statements and help them understand that if they disagree they need to tell you that or you will take it that they agree with you.

State the impact:

Finally show the void how their continued behaviour of withdrawal is affecting the people around them, start to appeal to the logic and relationship side of your argument. If the intent is more about justice show them how withdrawal is not fair on others, and if the intent is more about harmony, show them how their behaviour is causing frustration and potential conflict.

Actions to avoid:

- Don't jump in; you need to explore the intent first to understand where they are coming from.
- Push too fast, above all else you need to take your time with the void, never push for a quick resolution.
- Avoid losing your temper, stay calm and focused and talk it out with the void.

Bringing the best out of: **The Doomsayer**

Bringing the best out of: **The Doomsayer**

The Intent

The intent behind the doomsayer's behaviour is to get it right. They are focused on accuracy and want it to be 100% correct before they agree. Also they will pull your idea apart and pick out all the issues with it.

From their point of view:

If a job is worth doing it is worth doing right, this is the motto of the doomsayer; however, nothing is ever good enough for them. They can't understand how others cannot see the flaws in what they are suggesting. It is up to the doomsayer to point out the errors and shortcomings of other people's ideas. The doomsayer believes they are doing the right thing and being realistic, there is no point starting something that is not going to work.

How to deal with 'The Doomsayer':

Doomsayers focus on the 20% of an idea that will not work ignoring the 80% that is fine. They bring others down with them and discourage innovation and creativity. If you are faced with a doomsayer here is what you need to do:

1. Agree on negativity
2. Draw on their passion
3. Take your time
4. Beat them to it
5. Use their skills

Agree on negativity:

The worst thing you can do when engaging with a doomsayer is to try and convince them to try and focus on the positives.

This comes later, for now you need to agree with their negativity, allow them to be as negative as they want. Encourage them to tell you everything that is wrong with a situation or idea. Let them talk it out. Do not agree or disagree with their statements (remember you are agreeing with their negativity, not their comments). When they have finally started to slow down and reduce their negativity it is time to engage with their passion.

Draw on their passion:

The doomsayer is focused on accuracy, so engage with that. Once they have 'ranted' enough on what is wrong, start to explore what would be right in their opinion. Ask them what they would do differently and why, focus on the task and not the person. They are passionate about the right result so start to lead the conversation towards what the ideal outcome would be. While focusing on the outcome remind them of current limitations and resources. If they start to be overly negative again then ask them for alternatives.

Take your time:

Take your time when dealing with the doomsayer, they are 'wired' for seeing what will not work, or what is wrong, it will take time for them to acknowledge what is working or what elements are right. Get the doomsayer to explore options where they can work together with others to achieve the right result. Where they cannot agree to this then slowly bring the doomsayer towards a workable compromise, explaining the logic and rational to your suggestion.

Beat them to it:

A good suggestion when dealing with the doomsayer is to 'beat them to the punch' by identifying issues or problems upfront. By suggesting the negatives up front you may get them to respond with a positive statement (so they are picking out what is wrong with your statement), or at least they will agree with you. If you show that you are concerned about the accuracy of the work they will be more flexible in their approach.

Use their skills:

Finally, use the doomsayer for what they are best at, but use them to your advantage. Encourage them to identify problems and issues early in the process and ask them to suggest alternatives. Help others understand that they are attacking the problem not the person. Use language such as ' *thank you for pointing out these problems so we can come up with solutions*', and ' I *know you want this to be right so what can we do...*'. It may also be helpful to slightly adjust your attitude towards the doomsayer by:

Shift your attitude towards:

- Seeing the positive intent in their behaviour, after all they are just overly concerned with getting it right.
- It's not about getting them to stop finding fault with ideas or situations; it's about getting them to be constructive with their criticism.
- Look to acknowledge when they catch something before it has a negative impact on results.

Bringing the best out of: **The Whinger**

Bringing the best out of: **The Whinger**

The Intent

Remember the intent behind the behaviour of the whinger is to get it right, they believe that nothing around here is right and nobody cares about it either.

From their point of view:

The whinger truly believes that the world is against them, nobody cares and they have given up trying to do anything about it. All that is left to do is vent their frustrations on everybody else, after all it is these people that caused the problem in the first place. There is no point in trying to fix anything because there is too much to fix, so what is the point in starting, it won't make a difference overall.

How to deal with 'The Whinger':

Whingers can be very difficult to deal with, they complain about everything and everyone, if you are faced with a whinger here is what you need to do:

1. Let them blow off
2. Grab an issue
3. Ask for solutions
4. Vision of the future
5. Draw a line

Let them blow off:

While the whinger is 'blowing off steam' listen for the main points that they are complaining about. The last thing you may want to do is listen to more whinging but it is a critical step.

Let them complain for 1-2 minutes and try to listen to what they are saying; you will need to identify a specific area to focus on in the next step. It is important to keep your body language and facial gestures neutral while they are complaining, avoid becoming defensive or dismissive. Don't agree or disagree with the whinger, just let them talk.

Grab an issue:

After you have identified a specific area from their complaining grab hold of this area and interrupt them. A good way to interrupt is by saying their name (you may need to repeat this over and over until you get their attention). Once you have their attention ask them to be specific about what is wrong with this area/item. Be careful here, the whinger will want to go back to generic whinges, you need to keep pulling them toward the specific, for example, *'you said the meeting was a waste of time, specifically what part of the meeting was a waste of time?'*. Every time the whinger tries to backtrack to generics repeat the focus question to force them into specifics.

Ask for solutions:

Once you have them talking about a specific issue ask them what they would do to resolve it. Again be careful here as they won't want to look at solutions, they just want to whinge. Keep asking them what they would do to resolve it, what is their suggested solution to the issue. Do not offer any solutions yourself (the whinger will only complain about these!), focus solely on getting the whinger to generate solutions.

Vision of the future:

If they are unable or unwilling to look at solutions then try showing them a vision of the future. Create a perfect vision of the future by asking them a question like *'well in a year's time if everything was fixed what would it look like'*. When they describe what it would be like simply ask them *' ok, so what do we need to start doing now to create this future'*.

Draw a line:

If nothing you do can get the whinger to focus on solutions then it is time to draw the line and walk away. Do not express anger or frustration, simply state (assertively), *'I can't help you until you are willing to focus on solutions, when you want to look at ways we can fix this come and talk to me'*. This is not the ideal outcome but at least they will stop whinging at you. Even in the case of the world's most devoted whinger they will learn through your behaviours that it is pointless whinging at you.

Actions to avoid:

- Never agree or disagree with the whinger, it is about solutions, if you agree or disagree they will increase their level of complaining.
- Avoid offering solutions, the whinger will only start to complain about these also.
- Never confuse whinging with venting, the whinger complains non-stop all of the time. Venting is just letting off steam when things get too much for us.

Bringing the best out of: **The Controller**

Bringing the best out of: **The Controller**

The Intent

Remember the intent behind the behaviour of the controller is to get it done, they are focusing on results. They want it done now and have no problem stepping in and doing it themselves.

From their point of view:

The task is the most important thing, if other people are not ready to step in and do what is required the controller will. After all it does not matter who does it as long as it gets done. The controller can become impatient and frustrated at other people's lack of urgency towards a task. Sometimes a task needs their focus and urgency as it will never be completed without their control.

How to deal with 'The Controller':

The controller wants to control everything, from planning to delivery they will step in and take charge telling others what to do and how to do it. This behaviour can drive people mad when left unchecked. Here is a good strategy for dealing with the controller:

1. Acknowledge intent
2. Discuss the impact
3. Explore reasons
4. Agree ownership
5. Agree actions

Acknowledge intent:

Behind the difficult behaviour of the controller is a genuine positive intent to get results, they want to get it done now.

Acknowledge this positive intent, let the controller know you admire their commitment to the result. Use language such as *'I can see you are passionate about this'*, or *'I know how important this result is to you'*. Help them understand you are just as concerned and focused on the actual result.

Discuss the impact:

The controller may not be aware of the impact of their behaviour on others (they do not see it as a negative behaviour, after all they are just getting it done). You need to raise their awareness of the impact of their behaviour and how it is limiting the ability of others to achieve results. Use language that they understand to emphasise the impact, show them how their behaviours can cause inefficiency for others. Don't focus on the impact to people, focus on the impact to results, for example *'when you do... that means Joe cannot get...'*.

Explore reasons:

Work with the controller to identify the reasons behind their behaviour, why is it so urgent, why does it have to be done a specific way. Try to address their concerns and keep a focus on the result. Discuss the methods used and the impact on the result. Help them see the bigger picture and how their behaviour is limiting the overall result. If they have a specific issue with a person's ability then ask them *'what does this person need to do to improve'*, encourage them to act as a mentor and enable others to achieve the same level of productivity instead of jumping in and doing it for them.

Agree ownership:

Draw up a list of activities and discuss ownership of items. Make sure the controller clearly knows what they are and are not responsible for. Clearly state the consequences if they step over the agreed line in the future. Agree a process where the controller can raise concerns if they feel something is not getting the level of attention its urgency deserves, instead of them stepping in and taking control.

Agree actions:

Finally agree actions; who will do what and by when. Make sure it is clear who is responsible for the actions. Define a process for checking on progress and adherence. Controllers are very supportive of the quick 'traffic light' report where a RED item needs urgent attention, ORANGE is raising a concern but it is not a 'showstopper', and GREEN is everything is good with this aspect/item.

Actions to avoid:

- Never make it personal with the controller, they are not trying to undermine you, they just want to get it done.
- Don't confuse the controller with a 'political schemer', the schemer is trying to undermine you and get the credit for it (treat these people like a cross between the bully and the sniper).
- Don't ignore the controller's behaviour, sometimes it is easier to ignore them and just do it your way when they are not around, but this only encourages the difficult behaviour.

Bringing the best out of: **The Waster**

Bringing the best out of: **The Waster**

The Intent

The waster wants everyone to think they are so busy and indispensible; they like to be the centre of attention. This behaviour is driven by the intent to get appreciated, they want acknowledgement (not for what they do, but for who they are).

From their point of view:

The waster actually sees themselves as overworked, they truly believe they are 'up to their eyes' with work, however, they need to let everyone else know this, *'as in this place other people are always trying to offload their work on you'*. Unless you can show just how busy you are you will end up with twice as much work as before.

How to deal with 'The Waster':

The waster swans around telling everyone how busy they are and how important their work is, however they spend more time talking about work than actually doing it. If you need to deal with a waster here is a good strategy to tackle their behaviour:

1. Acknowledge commitment
2. Address results
3. Avoid excuses
4. Get commitments
5. Agree follow up

Acknowledge commitment:

Behind it all the waster is looking for appreciation, give it to them. Acknowledge the areas/task they are delivering on.

The issue you want to address is getting them to deliver more, take on more, or to at least stop going on about how much they think they are doing. Make it a habit of identifying what they are doing well. If you acknowledge their good intent this will reduce their need for others to acknowledge it. Make it clear from the initial discussion you want them to focus on doing things differently.

Address results:

Start to focus on output and results by asking them, how they can achieve more by doing it a different or more efficient way. Look for their input on this and be ready for a backlash of how busy they are and how much they are already doing. Again, keep your focus on the results, acknowledge areas in which they are doing well, and use these areas to draw them out and generate ideas how they can get better results elsewhere or on other aspects of their work. For example 'Joe, *you did a great job with the advertising on the Mitchell campaign, how could you get a similar result with the Jones's account*?'

Avoid excuses:

The waster will have 101 excuses as to why they can't deliver or who is holding them up. Resist the temptation to explore these excuses, instead simply ignore them by stating, '*I'm not asking you why you can't deliver, I need to know what you can do to deliver going forward...*' Every time they bring up an excuse ask them what they need to do to overcome this issue or obstacle.

Get commitments:

Turn the conversation towards actual commitments'. Ask the waster to define what they are going to do, how they are going to do it, and when they are going to do it. If they give a time line that you feel is too long, then redirect them by asking *'what would it take for you to do it by...'* Get the waster to document these commitments and use it to follow up with them.

Agree follow up:

Finally agree how and when you will follow up to review their progress. Use the documented commitments they produced as the guideline for the follow up meeting. If they start to make more excuses when you meet for the follow up start over again from step 3 (avoiding excuses). If needed clearly state the consequences to the waster if they continue to fail to deliver on their commitments.

Actions to avoid:

- Don't threaten the waster up front, try to appeal to their good intent before showing them what will happen if they fail to deliver.
- Avoid getting bogged down with all their excuses, they will have an endless supply, simply redirect them back to the actual results required and what they are going to do about it.
- Never agree with their negative opinions of other people, keep the focus on what they will do, not what others are not doing.

Chapter Ten: The Final Word

Removing the barriers to your success

10

The Final Word

A summary of the key steps in understanding DiSC and difficult people, remember to embrace the three A's acknowledge, accept, and appreciate the differences between you and everyone else. By deepening your understanding you will increase your success.

Our journey through this book has brought us from DISC to dealing with difficult people. Along the way we explored behaviours, intent, impact, and strategies for success. Now that you have reached the final chapter it is time to reflect on the key information contained within this book.

The previous chapter has provided you with a range of strategies to successfully deal with the *'Dirty Dozen'* of unwanted behaviours. However, it is not about the strategies alone, they need to be used in conjunction with a deeper understanding of DISC and difficult behaviours. Here is what you need to remember when dealing with difficult people:

DISC – key points

- We are never just a D, I, S or C, we are a blend of all four behavioural styles.
- Everyone is different, we need to embrace this.
- When under pressure we tend to increase our primary DISC behaviour style.
- The D-Style is fast paced and task focused.
- The I-Style is fast paced and people focused.
- The S-Style is steady paced and people focused.
- The C-Style is steady paced and task focused.
- DISC is a 3-step model of understanding self, understanding others and adapting for success.

The DISC Model

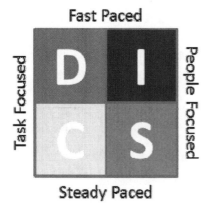

The basic model works across two dimensions. The first dimension looks at your pace, either fast-paced or steady-paced. The second dimension looks at your focus, either task focused or people focused. Depending on your pace and focus this will direct you towards D, I, S or C.

A quick summary of the four styles of DiSC:

D –Dominance

We can describe a person who is fast-paced and task focused as a high D for dominance. A high D can be described as:

- *Results orientated*
- *Goal focused*
- *Action orientated*
- *Decisive and direct*

A person with a high D factor likes to achieve results, has a desire to take control, and is very competitive. They are very comfortable accepting challenges, they can be strong willed and impatient. They are quick to take action and are very innovative. High D's have a tendency to love power and authority, they are also motivated by direct answers. They may have high egos and drive hard for results. They like challenges and are natural problem solvers. Their strong focus on results may be seen by others as overly aggressive behaviour and some D's may be described as being a bully or being to directive when dealing with others.

I –Influence

We can describe a person who is fast-paced and people focused as a high I for influence. A high I can be described as:

- *People orientated*
- *Optimistic and encouraging*
- *Enthusiastic and open*
- *Expressive and outgoing*

A person with a high I factor likes to receive recognition and praise; they are influential and enthusiastic about their tasks and goals. They may be described as very entertaining and expressive; they can be very talkative and enjoy dealing with people. High I's can be described as socially and verbally aggressive, they are energising and help motivate others. A high I can be seen as overly dependent on interaction with other people and seem overly needy of recognition and praise.

S –Steadiness

We can describe a person who is steady paced and people focused as a high S for steadiness. A high S can be described as:

- *Stable and cooperative*
- *Good listener, sympathetic*
- *Good team worker, dependable*
- *Diplomatic and consistent*

A person with a high S factor likes to avoid conflict and will always seek harmony. They can be described as very loyal to those they identify with. They are good listeners and very patient of others. They dislike rapid or constant change preferring instead to focus on security and stability.

They like to work within a predictable environment where traditional and steady procedures are adopted. They have an orientation towards family activities and values. They may procrastinate over decision-making and will avoid giving constructive feedback.

C –Conscientiousness

We can describe a person who is steady paced and task focused as a high C for conscientiousness. A high C can be described as:

- *Analytical and accurate*
- *Orderly and disciplined*
- *Quality conscious*
- *Deliberate and systematic*

A person with a high C factor likes to reflect on situations before taking action. They want to analyse the facts and figures or pros and cons of the situation before making a decision. They are objective thinkers with a tendency to be perfectionists. They set high standards and are well disciplined in delivering accurate results in line with expectations, processes, and/or procedures. They are motivated by the right way to proceed, and will always seek justice in a given situation. The high C's may be seen as cold and withdrawn by others.

Remember the 3'A's

1. Acknowledge: people are different. Not everyone sees the world the same way you see it.
2. Accept: just because they are different does not make it wrong, it is just different. Remember they are looking at you and saying the same thing.
3. Appreciate: thankfully people are different, this gives us a richness of diversity and allows us to explore these differences to reach greater successes thorough understanding.

Reading people's behaviour

Remember to use the following guide when trying to diagnose someone's behaviour style:

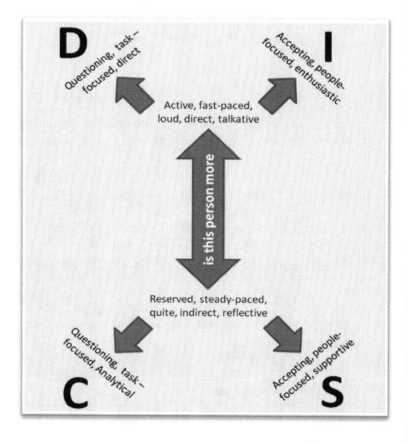

Be aware that we can all display different behaviours depending on the situation and/or our frame of mind. Look at typical behaviours over the course of time for a better understanding of a person's behavioural style.

Try to understand before passing judgement:

We can all have a different perception of the same thing. Remember to seek to understand the other person's point of view before you judge them or try to enforce your point of view.

Look for the positive intent:

When dealing with difficult people and behaviours, remember to look for the positive intent behind their behaviour, select your approach and communication steps and finally apply the correct strategy for bringing the best out of these people:

Understand the intent:

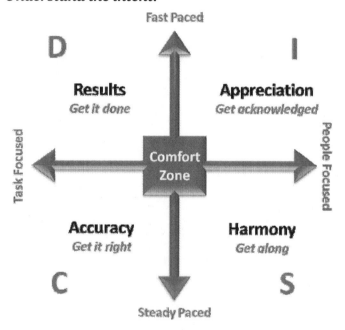

Use the 5-step approach:

1. Reduce barriers and differences
2. Listen closely to understand
3. Explore and understand
4. Communicate clearly
5. Focus on the positive and improvement